To my new friend

# 31

## Steps To Your

# Millions

## In Antiques &
## Collectibles

### *The Best Kept Secrets Revealed*

by
Daryle S. Lambert

**31 Steps to Your Millions in Antiques & Collectibles**

May, 2007 First Edition, First Printing
By Daryle S. Lambert
ISBN: 978-0-9796423-0-2

For information, contact 31 Inc. at www.31corp.com.

Printed in the United States of America

Author: Daryle S. Lambert
Senior Editor/Layout Director: Clarke F. Echols, Sr.
Technical Advisor/Art Director: Chris Erbach
Assistant Editors: Gail Glasser, Vickie Lambert, Cindy Nieder

Visit our web site:
www.31corp.com

Printed 2007 in the United States of America

From Daryle

# Dedication

*To my wonderful wife Vickie*
*and my children*
*Daryle II, Dana, Lawson, Landon and Joshua.*
*I love you and always will.*
*Thanks to each one of you*
*for your patience*
*and encouragement.*

# Contents

## Part II

## Real Stories of Real Treasure Hunters in the Real World
## of Antiques, Collectibles, and Fine Works of Art

**Part VII**

**Returning Home: The End of A Voyage**

**The Beginning of A New Dream**

# <u>Acknowledgments</u>

## From Daryle

My thanks to the greatest team in the world. They enabled me to bring this book to the marketplace. I truly hope this book will be one to benefit the readers who take it to heart.

I would be remiss if I didn't thank God for giving me the ability and life events to share with you in this book. I thank Him with my whole heart.

My wife, Vickie and my son, Joshua, have shown great patience and understanding during the many long hours and evenings apart from family activities it has taken to complete this book. Joshua, I am truly sorry for the games I missed while writing. Vickie, I sure appreciate you for taking over so many of the tasks around the house, and I am so very grateful for your support. I thank you both with all I am.

My thanks to my friends, Cindy Nieder and Gail Glasser. Without their encouragement to put my pen to paper, this book would still be only a few scraps of hand written notes on my shelf. Often, when I would lay aside my writing, one of them would call and encourage me forward. I have been able to depend on Cindy for her keen insight, writing knowledge, and skill in merchandising this book.

From encourager to right-hand-woman, Gail has been my Queen-Of-All-Trades. She simply amazes me with her enthusiasm and her ability to jump right in there and get done whatever I need without hesitation, whether it is business or personal.

Clarke F. Echols, Sr. was able to take a writer with no professional experience and mold his words into a book that will be helpful to many. Often, he would call and ask what I really meant on a certain page, then he'd E-mail me the way it would better read. I will never be able to fully thank him for the many hours of hard work he has put into this book. The great thing about being connected with Clarke is the many wonderful stories we've shared together as the book was being written.

My good friend Warner Smith's introduction to Chris Erbach has made it possible to bring my manuscript to life. Chris has been the glue that has stuck our team together. Always quiet, yet always listening, his diligence, high standards, and technical savvy has produced an outstanding design, for both our book and web site, and has enabled the technical parts of the book to come together.

I call Chris, Clarke, Cindy, Gail, Vickie, and Joshua, my "Nothing Is Impossible Team." Nothing I have asked them to do has proven to be impossible for them.

And I am blessed by them.

# A Letter From the Author

*Dear Reader,*

*I would like to extend an invitation to you to cast aside your cares and join me on an exciting journey. Indeed, it could even become a life-changing* **adventure**.

*The rewards that await you are unimaginable until you experience them for yourself. I promise you that your life will never be the same once you have set out on this magnificent expedition.*

*I can make that promise because it has been true for so many others I have helped to set sail on their own respective paths of excitement, challenge and suspense.*

*Many years ago, I began this same journey myself. The rewards have been so great that I still wake up each and every morning, eager to get started on another adventurous day. Because I have found it so rewarding, I want to see others be able to enjoy it too.*

*Jesus taught: Of him to whom much is given, much is required.*

*Now, as I enter into those wonderful years some call the "Golden Years" of my mortal experience, I feel a duty to pass my knowledge and experience on to others who will follow me on their new path of life. They can benefit from the knowledge that I have acquired through many years of trial and error. This should make their journey much easier.*

*An old proverb says, "Give a man a fish and you feed him for a day. Teach him to fish, and he can feed himself for the rest of his life." I like to add one word to that adage: ". . .Teach a man to* **CATCH** *fish, and he can feed himself for the rest of his life."*

*The purpose of this book is to help you learn to catch fish — even some big ones in due time — instead of just dangling a hook in the water, hoping something might bite before it snags on a tree root.*

*My objective in inviting you on this journey is not to help* you make a living. You already have an occupation or a job to do that. Instead, I am here to help you become wealthy. Then, if you choose, you can have the option of continuing in your current occupation, or pursuing something entirely different, if that is what you prefer.

I can help you best by sharing part of myself with you. I'll be relating stories from my life's experiences to help you understand how I did many of the things I did in the antiques and collectible market, rather than just telling you what to do.

And because my life is made richer by those around me, I will also be telling you about some of their experiences so you can benefit from their accomplishments as well. In fact, I might even go so far as to admit how, on one occasion, my mistake put a very nice profit in a friend's pocket when it could have been my own. That way, you can avoid making a similar error.

So come. Join me in the adventure. Bon voyage!

Best regards,
Daryle

# Foreword

This is a book about you. It is a book about how you can combine a set of basic principles in your life with your energy and interests, to create a degree of personal financial independence. Then, if you desire, you can carry the same process forward until you become comfortably wealthy. It is a book about how to add value to yourself, your efforts, and your time, so you can permanently escape from what many call "the daily grind," if that is what you want. Or it can enable you to do what you love without having to be concerned about the financial issues of life.

Within these pages, you will learn how to properly apply those principles to produce rewards that are quite substantial, given an appropriate period of time. These principles do not involve trying to "beat the system" or to manipulate a market or other people. They are always centered on doing what is right, what is honest and ethical, and in delivering solid value to anyone you might be doing business with.

Albert Einstein said, *"Try not to become a man of success, but rather to become a man of value."*

As you unlock the secrets in this book, you will discover some important differences between methods sometimes used by others, but which often do not work, and building a solid basis for your own financial accomplishment using sound principles based on honesty, integrity, and value.

The world is full of many opportunities. All you need to do is discover where your interests lie, find a suitable vehicle compatible with your interests and values, develop the necessary skills and knowledge, then set out in pursuit of what you desire.

Contrary to what many claim, it does not take money to make money. Using the principles taught within these pages, you can take as little as a few dollars and, through a series of transactions, convert that into a growing reserve of cash that you can reinvest to grow it into a very real personal fortune, all without incurring any debt, by always using money that is your own.

We each have only one life to live. Live it wisely because life is not a dress rehearsal.

Now let's toss the cares of the world aside, and take a journey together into the territory of what could be, and discover the precious treasures hidden in your future, that are waiting for you to uncover them.

*William S. Horton (1865 - 1936)*

# Part I

## Chapter 1

### The Birth of a Life-Long Dream

When I was a small boy in Owensboro, Kentucky, I read Robert Louis Stevenson's classic novel, *Treasure Island*. That single book set the stage for what I would do for the rest of my life.

Every day my heart is filled with gratitude for that wonderful book and how it captured my imagination. It set me on a course of adventure and challenge I still travel today, decades later, at the exciting age of sixty-five.

The wonderful thing about this adventure is that you are never too old, nor too young, to begin it. Even as a young child, I went on treasure hunts, although others thought I was crazy. My treasure hunts were in the form of collecting coins and stamps, and many other things that captured my interest. I had an unquenchable thirst to find something special – something others might have overlooked, or thought had no value.

Looking for treasures every day and being willing to invest in them can be indescribably rewarding. It can also produce very unexpected results. My coin collection did just that.

As a child, collecting coins brought me many hours of pure joy, as I filled each page in my coin books with those precious metallic specimens. Year after year, I would go to my room and marvel at the rare pieces that were now mine now because of my persistence in seeking and finding them.

Often, when others were playing ball or watching television, I was traveling back and forth, to and from the bank with my heavy bags of coins. Four or five times a week, I made a trip to the local bank, bought a bag of coins, and sifted through them. Each bag of rejected coins went back to the bank, where I traded it for another bag to search through. There were times I returned a whole bag of coins, never finding a single one I wanted to keep.

One of life's great secrets is that if a positive activity is repeated over and over, the results usually come out positive in the end. In this instance, merely by looking at enough coins, I was certain to find a few that would enhance my collection. I still find this type of dedication useful today as I continue in my search to discover new treasures.

Even when I was young, I was searching for that "treasure" and found it. This collection truly became an important resource when those once common coins finally evolved, years later, into a very useful asset when I needed it most. My persistence in collecting coins turned into a tangible asset over the years.

You can't imagine my surprise when at eighteen years old, already married with a wife and child to support, and wanting to go to college, I discovered that the coin collection I'd accumulated grew in value over the years until it became sufficient enough to pay for my entire college education at Kentucky Wesleyan College.

I was rewarded with the great personal satisfaction, knowing my parents would not have to be burdened with supporting my family while I finished my college education. I was further rewarded knowing that I had done this myself. I also knew I wouldn't be leaving school with mountains of debt – so much debt that I would struggle for years just to barely survive, like so many others I knew.

This new reality gave me the comfort and satisfaction of knowing I was successful in my own right, with no need to depend on others for my family's well-being. It was exciting to know *if I dreamed* big enough dreams, *all my desires* could come true. This was reassuring to a person so young, as I was, and it gave me confidence that *nothing was beyond my reach*. All the wonderful things this country has to offer were there — right in front of me — and I enthusiastically dove, head-first, into my dreams.

I won't say these were easy times in my life, but they shaped and prepared me for the adventures that lay ahead. I wasn't sure where my dreams would lead me, but I was certain I did not want to wait any longer to begin the adventure.

### Another Seed is Planted

After college, still searching for that "treasure" and always knowing it could be just around the next corner as long as I didn't give up, I chose to follow my dad into the oil business. I had heard about the "gushers" — oil wells found in Texas — where the oil came flowing out of the ground, even without a pump, and how people became very wealthy as a result — wealthy beyond their wildest imaginations.

This thought takes me back in time to when I was a young child. I marveled at the big cars people drove and the large homes others lived in. One of my favorite memories is of the time when I was about 10 years old.

My very good friend, Bruce Embry, showed up at my house one day with a big surprise. The sparkle and excitement in his eyes told me he had something important to tell me. Sure enough, his Uncle Jim had just called. This instantly hinted of a chance we might be going to the ball park. His uncle Jim Ellis thought the world of Bruce, and enjoyed taking him to baseball games whenever it was convenient. I was often invited along, so I was anxiously hoping this would be one of those afternoons.

Jim Ellis was quite wealthy, but at the time I had little understanding of what being wealthy meant. Like most families after the war, my family was struggling. My dad was employed making Popsicles at a plant in Kentucky, and there was no hint that 10 years later he would be involved in the oil business as owner of his own company. I later learned that Bruce's uncle Jim had made his money from oil production.

Bruce asked my parents if I could join him and his Uncle Jim for another baseball game at the park. The requisite parental approval secured, Bruce, Jim, and I went to watch the Owensboro Oilers, a farm club for the New York Yankees, play Class D Kitty-League baseball. [Two famous players, Harold "Pee Wee" Reese and Joe DiMaggio played in an exhibition game between the Brooklyn Dodgers and the New York Yankees in Owensboro in 1940 (the Dodgers won, 10-6). There were many other superstars in that game as well.]

After arriving at the ball park, Uncle Jim asked the two of us if we would like a soda and popcorn. Just like any red-blooded American ten-year-old would, we enthusiastically approved the suggestion. But little did I know how much my life would be affected by what happened next.

### A Life Is Changed

As the vendor passed us our refreshments, Uncle Jim reached into the pocket of his bib overalls and pulled out a large roll of one-hundred-dollar bills. I was mesmerized. I had never seen a hundred-dollar bill before, but instantly I knew I wanted to be able to do what he had done — pull out a wad of high dollar cash. I figured he certainly must have found his own treasure somewhere.

Even at the very unripe, young age of ten, I was training my mind to focus on the things that made others success-ful, so I could apply this knowledge later in my life. Ask-ing questions came easy for me — even in my early years — and I never failed to take the opportunity to question how successful people made their money. You see, I knew anyone who had become as successful as Uncle Jim must have set himself above the average working person, and I wanted to know how he did that.

Later, after he took us home, I asked Bruce where his uncle made his money. Bruce told me his Uncle Jim owned a large num-ber of farmland acreages scattered throughout several states that he had bought during the Great De-pression at very inexpensive prices. Years later, oil was discovered on many of them, and while everyone else was struggling, he was accu-mulating a huge fortune.

>> Clue 1

There is always a correct time to take those actions that will result in your success. If you don't take advantage of op-portunities when they appear, the wait for the next one may be years away.

There is always a correct time to take those actions that will result in your success. If you don't take advantage of opportunities when they appear, the wait for the next one may be years away. Buying the farms when everyone else was selling proved to be the secret to Uncle Jim's fortune.

I carefully stored that information away in my mind be-cause I knew it would become very useful at a later date. It is amazing to think about this today in the year 2007 when the price of oil has gone as high as $80 dollars per barrel, and contrast that with when Uncle Jim sold most of his oil below two dollars per barrel. Yet he still accumulated one of the largest fortunes in the country.

### When "Gushers" Appear

When the value of our belongings change, often when we don't even know it or we least expect it, it can prove to be the very thing that gets us where we want to go. In the case of Jim, he never expected that farmland to be good for anything other than farming — that is, until the oil was discovered.

Back during the 1930's and 1940's, Jim used the same principles I will be teaching you in this book; namely, when you buy something, be sure its present value is worth the purchase price. You should also know that the possibility exists that any item could gain additional value for different reasons, and you may not even be aware of it at the time of the purchase. If the value is there at the start, any additional value added later makes it that much better, and you should be very thankful for it.

What a treasure it is when you strike oil where it has never been discovered before. I can say this from my own personal experience. Can you imagine finding something that was formed a very long time ago, just waiting to be discovered by someone, and that someone might be us?

I can recall many times sitting on the floor of a drilling rig as we approached the depth where it was assumed oil would be found. My heart would beat a mile-a-minute with pure excitement.

Once in Kentucky, as I was waiting for that special moment when the drillers announced they thought they had found oil, it seemed as if I was in a dream. After many hours of waiting for the test, a gusher came spurting upward. The oil rose over 200 feet in the air, flowing at a rate of 800 barrels a day. In Kentucky, a well that size is definitely a treasure, by any standard.

Today, when I visit the farm where this particular well was first drilled and oil discovered, I always receive a warm handshake and big hugs from the owners of the farm, Mr. & Mrs. Payne. Last year, Mr. Payne told me he still receives over $100,000 per year from his royalty income consisting of one-eighth of all the oil still being produced on his farm. You see, by allowing the well to be drilled on his land, he was promised he would own one-eighth of all the oil produced as a "royalty," all at no expense to himself.

### Joining the World of Real Estate

When the price of oil dropped in the 1970's, I decided to try my hand at real estate, partly because it was costing more to produce the oil than it was selling for at the time. I read all the books about how the real estate business was growing, and it seemed to be a suitable field to pursue in my ongoing search for new treasure.

I formed my own real estate company and soon had over 15 brokers on the payroll, leaving me no time to continue searching for the things that really brought me satisfaction. I was too busy taking care of every one else's needs plus the needs of their families, and it was time to turn my attention back to the needs of my own family. Besides, the business I "owned" had reached the point where it owned me, and every day was feeling too much like "work". I realized I would far rather be searching for treasures than listing and selling real estate.

### How about Stocks and Bonds?

I put all my properties up for sale and prepared for my next life changing adventure. I was still a young man in my thirties, so I decided to try my hand at finding treasure by becoming a stockbroker.

In the late 1970's, while living in Kentucky, I formed a trading firm and began trading stocks. To this day, I still trade stocks and enjoy it very much. Once in a while, I still find a stock I believe has the potential to become a true treasure.

During my stockbroker days, I was sharpening my skills

and formulating my plan — the plan I will be showing you later in the book. After about ten years of running the securities firm I founded, I no longer had the desire to invest in the markets or run a company of my own. I found you could never be correct all the time for your clients and, unfortunately, that was what most of them expected. I wanted to do something I could do alone, with just myself to answer to and depend upon.

It seemed to me that as I became successful in business and as my companies grew, my interest in them waned. I have spent many hours trying to figure out why this loss of interest occurred, and the best explanation I can come up with is that as I hired more people, I had less time for the real things that held my interest.

## Let's Try Commodities Trading. . .

So, off to Chicago I went where I began to trade commodities at the Chicago Board of Trade. Now that is a fast paced life! I saw more money made and lost in a shorter period of time than you could ever imagine. I had finally found something I think just might have been even too fast for me.

## No Place Like Home

Seeking a slower pace in life, I retired from the Board of Trade and am now a very happy stay-at-home father of a wonderful eight-year-old son. I had always heard the best things in life come to those who wait, and I can positively affirm it is certainly true for me.

Although taking care of Joshua is pretty much a full-time job that keeps me on my toes, I continue to invest in fine art and collectibles. I don't seem to get enough of hunting for treasure. Buying and selling these wonderful treasures is exciting and something I will never give up.

My son, Joshua, has been attending estate sales and auctions with me since he was six months old. I would carry him in a "snuggy," a sling-like pouch, on my chest, and often we would go to estate sales, antique sales, and auctions together. He has grown up learning to identify special pieces among the common or trash, until he now knows one from the other. I have no doubt he will be a treasure hunter one day, just like his father. His train and toy gun collections are already beginning to take over our house, and he definitely enjoys sharing them with his friends.

Every time we bring home a new piece for Josh's collection, my wife gives us the same warning: If you buy another thing I will throw it away. But of course she never does, and I think secretly she enjoys seeing Joshua's excitement with each new find as much as I do.

Every day I have the opportunity to talk to many wonderful people about some of the most beautiful things ever made by man. I find most people are proud of the things they collect, and enjoy sharing them with others, as do I. From all my years

*Living with Your Treasures.*

of buying and selling these treasures, I have also been able to build my own collection of beautiful pieces of pottery, porcelain, glass and paintings. When people come into our home, they comment about my beautiful collection of treasures. Most people have never been exposed to these valuable rarities, and I find great pleasure in showing them the wonderful pieces I have discovered in my quest.

### A Yearning to Explore the Unknown

Throughout my sixty-five years, one constant has been an unending yearning to explore the unknown. No matter what I worked at, in the back of my mind, there was still the desire to find those things of special value that others may have overlooked.

I inherited that feeling of yearning from my father. When I was growing up, he left Kentucky for a short time and went to live in Wyoming to prospect for uranium. He received several hundred-thousand acres in mineral rights from the government Office of Land Management, which was no small feat. It also proved to be a considerable windfall for our family and another completed adventure for my Dad.

So, perhaps it is easy to understand how my tremendously compulsive personality was formed. I married Joshua's mother, Vickie in 1982 and fortunately for me, she shares in my passion for collecting treasures. We work together locating beautiful paintings and pieces of art glass, and even if she won't admit it to me, she is as proud of our collections as I am. I can see it in her eyes and hear it in her voice as she shows our guests each new piece we have acquired, and handles them so lovingly.

Although I hate to admit it, Vickie may be better at discovering a treasure than I am. She definitely has a better eye for those special things we are looking for to add to our collections.

Starting in the 1980's, and continuing more than two decades, right up to the present time, I have been learning the skills of a collector and dealer in fine art and collectibles. As you no doubt can tell from reading this far, I have definitely been on a treasure hunt most of my life, and hope to continue this journey for many more years. This desire to find treasure has taken me to most of the 50 states, as well as several foreign countries.

Even though I have owned many successful businesses in my working life, the one vocation that has always brought me the greatest pleasure and joy has been collecting. I don't know how long I will be on this earth, but I do know I will never stop looking. In fact, I believe there will even be greater treasures found in heaven, and I have little me is there searching for them now.

doubt my Dad is there searching for them now. Enough about me. Let's start setting the stage for your adventure into the land of treasure hunting. I am sure that in a short period of time you will be sharing your own stories with me.

*Maxwell Armfield (1882 - 1972)*

# Chapter 2

## Deciding On a Path to Explore

I explored various options and ways I could search for and find treasures that would be sufficiently rewarding to justify the effort required. I decided upon antiques and collectibles because searching for these types of items yields unlimited possibilities for finding that special piece that will bring the desired financial reward. There are many, many treasures just waiting to be found — if you are willing to just go out and look for them.

Treasures with your name written all over them can be found at the next house sale or sitting in the corner of your neighbors garage. If you just take the time to look, you would be amazed at what you might find. I have searched for many treasures in my life, and have discovered many places where they still can be found. This is part of what I want to share with you — the reader — to help you find your own possessions of great value.

Interestingly enough, luck plays no part in the plan I am revealing to you. If you simply follow each step as it is laid out, the rewards can be much greater than almost any other opportunity you have ever encountered. After all, where else can so little cash — perhaps only $100 or less — be turned into so much. Millions of dollars in a relatively short time is possible if you are persistent. In as little as five years, you could possibly meet all your financial dreams, but the wonderful thing about this plan is you can continue to follow it for the rest of your life if you desire.

>> **Clue 2**

Working for someone else will always mean they reap greater financial rewards as a result of your labor than you ever can. If you are an employee, take a moment to observe whether you are living as well as the owners of the business. *Probably not.*

If the idea of a very modest investment bringing big rewards interests you, then the only remaining question you must answer for yourself is, are you willing to do what is required to fulfill all of your dreams? The principles taught in this book never change, and you can use them as long as you desire, or until have accomplished enough that you no longer want to dream.

As you delve into the pages that follow, I hope you will absorb their thoughts and ideas like a sponge, and that these insights will set you on the course to be an exceptional person in whatever business you choose to pursue. I have found that I am much happier if I am working for myself.

Working for someone else will always mean they reap

greater financial rewards as a result of your labor than you ever can. If you are an employee, take a moment to observe whether you are living as well as the owners of the business. *Probably not.*

## Where Are You Going With Your Life?

For over 25 years, I have watched people trying to make enough money to retire on while living a comfortable lifestyle, yet they consistently fail to reach that objective. Sometimes they just can't make enough money regardless of their skills or opportunity. Sometimes other events outside their control block their progress.

But, even if you are financially careful, what constitutes a comfortable lifestyle means different things to different people. You will no doubt agree that being financially comfortable certainly should include peace of mind.

Most of us have worked long and hard during our lives and, though we have gotten by, we have never really gotten ahead. We have taken care of our families, put the kids through college, and maybe even have a little nest egg put away. But we still are usually a small accident or so away from real trouble.

Wouldn't it be nice to not have to worry about where the next car payment is coming from? Can you imagine not having to worry about checking your bank balance before buying something fun?

So how do we attain this peace of mind and financial security? Working for someone else will only make them better off, not you. For many, if not most workers, by the time we reach that milestone in life where we want to relax and enjoy the "golden years", as they are sometimes called, there may be no quality time left to pursue the things we had so yearned to do, due to factors outside our control.

A personal goal of yours may be to become financially secure, to not worry about your retirement funds or the fact that there might be health concerns in the future that might cost more than you can afford. Or maybe you want to provide a better lifestyle for your family or to be able to send your children to college.

### Is Money Evil?

Many people think they are quoting the New Testament when they say, "Money is the root of all evil."

That is not true. The Apostle Paul actually said, "The love of money is the root of all evil," which is a much more accurate statement. In truth, it is the way in which we use money that counts. Money is only an object that represents the right to purchase goods or services. Money is a basic need in our lives to accomplish the things that are important to us.

What is important to keep in mind is that as your wealth grows, you have an obligation to think about others, be of service to them where you can, and most importantly, remain humble. Always be thankful for all you receive. You are only given so many years on this earth and how you use them will determine your successes or failures. And if you are inclined to think of the important matters related to Eternity, you will also recognize that we are accountable to our Creator for what we do with our time, our means, and our opportunities in this life.

### Discipline: A Prerequisite to Success

The principles explained in this book provide the guidelines you will need to be successful in your quest to reach your highest goals, but you will have to remain disciplined in your search and in your efforts if you expect to reap the rewards. There is a very fine line between stellar success and abject failure, and part of my intent here is to help you become aware of where that dividing line is.

The reason most people fail miserably in their endeavors is they have no discipline (meaning self control or a plan) to sustain them in their search for the future they vaguely wish they could have.

When you finish reading this book, you will be able to formulate your own plan for a successful future. The discipline to form the plan and execute it must come from within you, as I mentioned earlier. Nobody else can do it for you. Once you begin your search, you must not waiver from your goal until it is reached.

This goal can be whatever you choose: A little spending money, a few thousand dollars, one million dollars, ten million dollars, or perhaps even $30 million dollars or more. However, you will never achieve these levels of accomplishment if you cannot visualize yourself there — as a millionaire or a multi-millionaire.

The reason most people never become leaders is they are unable to envision themselves in a position of power or influence, even if that power or influence could be used for accomplishing much good in the lives of others.

The same is true for becoming just plain wealthy: Most people can't see themselves living as a wealthy person, and thus they likely never will.

> **>> Clue 3**
>
> Most people never become leaders because they are unable to envision themselves in a position of power or influence, even if that power or influence could be used for accomplishing much good in the lives of others.
>
> The same is true for becoming just plain wealthy: Most people can't see themselves living as a wealthy person, and thus they likely never will.

Once you begin your quest toward the top, there must be no turning back. The train has left the station and anything that would hold you back must be left behind. If you don't turn around and look back, you will never again see the things that might hold you back, perpetually preventing you from fulfilling your dreams.

### Desire: The Driving Force of Life

Soon I will outline the steps for your success, but remember, it will be up to you to create enough desire to follow those steps and not be detoured from your chosen goal until it has been achieved in full. Dale Earnhart, the great race-car driver, said, "Coming in second only makes you the first loser."

A half-measure of success is not success the way I look at it. Once you have set your goals, be sure you are prepared to stay the course until they are achieved. If you stop before all your goals are met, often you will fall back into the clutches of just having a job.

There are many examples of people who had the desire to reach for the stars when others were trying to discourage them. Take for example J. Paul Getty, who took his lunch to work every day in a brown paper bag. Sam Walton drove the same old pickup truck, even after he was worth millions. Both of these men had a dream, and they never let others interfere with their plan or change their direction in life.

When the nay-sayers around them were being critical, Getty and Walton kept to the task of fulfilling their dreams. Discipline was simply a way of life for both of these men, and their successes demonstrate that each was able to stay the course until success was achieved.

Getty and Walton, and many like them, aren't very different than you or me; that is, until they developed their plans and turned them into a reality. Had they not followed their plan, they would have just melted into the crowd like most others. Both these men have become household legends while their critics have been left in the dust.

### What's Holding You Back?

Ask yourself this question: *"Why not me?"*

The only answer is that you haven't started your own personal search for success. Is the fear of failure holding you back? Have you listened to so many people who said you couldn't do it that you have begun to believe them?

There are many distractions along the road to success. Friends and family are the two most often mentioned reasons for people failing to fulfill their dreams. This may come as a great surprise to you, but it shouldn't, because we assume friends and family are on our side, right?

Although most of your friends wish you the best, they inwardly fear that if you are successful, you will move on without them. So they advise you to be very cautious as they continue plodding along in their everyday job. Their job, working for someone else, makes them happy and pays their bills. But I can assure you, every one of them is wishing they had a way out.

Your family is fearful you might get hurt if you venture out on your own, so they might try to hold you back for your own sake. What they don't understand is that you are adventurous, and long to see and experience how the other half lives. Both your friends and family believe they want only the best for you, but in doing so they can become barnacles on the hull of your ship of success, holding you back, and dragging you down.

Regardless of what others think or say, you must always be true to yourself and to your dreams. You were created by God with special gifts he designed only for you. It is up to you to use these gifts in such a way that they will bring you fulfillment as you bring blessings to the lives of those around you.

Others can never really know what you want out of life, and only through showing them, by example, will they fully understand where your future is headed.

## What Can I Best Do for Others?

I have found that the most wonderful thing you can do for others is to achieve the highest amount of success your talents afford you. As others witness your success they will say to themselves, "If he can do it, why can't I ?"

There are many ways to succeed in this world, and the best part of this plan I am about to lay out for you is that you don't have to change the way you are living, or the things you are doing that are important in your life, in order to be successful. You can still spend quality time with your family and friends, watch sports on television and even go fishing with your children.

I will show you examples of times when I was out with my family, yet still managed to find a treasure or two. My plan for success won't jeopardize your responsibility to your family, nor will it get in the way of your job. However, I do hope that at some point you will be able to stop being chained to the workplace.

## Be Careful About Where You Get Advice

It seems everybody and his friend has an idea about how you can become wealthy. There are innumerable books and expensive newsletters on the subject, instructing you how to invest your money or telling you that by changing the things you are doing now, you will become rich. The trouble is, usually the only person getting rich is the one writing the book or newsletter on how to get rich.

I recently read a book by a person who tells his readers if they work a minimum of fifty hours per week and follow his advice, they could become rich. However, after doing the math, I figured out that if I followed what he wanted me to do, I would be making only about $50,000 per year.

What will $50,000 per year buy you? First you have to pay the income and social-security taxes. That's about $15,000. The remainder is enough to pay the monthly mortgage payments, utilities, and upkeep on a house worth about $150,000 or maybe $200,000. Not bad but not great. Add in the money needed for gas, car payments, food, insurance, and any other basic expenses. There isn't much left for your peace of mind. And fifty hours per week is more than you are working now. This didn't sound like a very good plan to me.

$50,000 is a far cry from the wealth I have in mind. I doubt it is the "fortune" you had in mind either. It seems the road to success in that author's way of thinking is through a new job and a lot of overtime. While many people are looking for more money, few are looking for more overtime on their current job or at a second job.

The trouble with that author's plan for success is you are left at the starting point, selling low-valued items until you're burned out. Discouraged and out of energy, you eventually give up your dream. If this is your desire, my plan won't be for you. I want you to work less and make more. This process will soon take you from selling the cheaper and more common merchandise as you acquire experience, toward selling the top rarities where the real money can be made, once you master the basics.

What's important to understand — and it is a cornerstone of my plan — is that your knowledge increases as you hunt for your treasure. As it increases, you will become more interested in searching for the more expensive and rare items.

You cannot make a huge fortune by selling $5 items. When you sell exclusively inexpensive things that have only small dollar value, you must make a huge number of sales and transactions to turn enough cash to overcome expenses, leaving very little or no profit. Consequently, your dream of financial success will become lost in the mud from the hassles of moving nickel-and-dime items.

> **>> Clue 4**
>
> It can take as much time and effort to sell a $5 item as it does to sell a $10,000 item. If your profit on that $5 item is 100% of cost, you made $5, but if your profit on an item you bought for $10,000 is also 100% of your initial investment, you pocket $10,000. Which would you prefer?

It can take as much time and effort to sell a $5 item as it does to sell a $10,000 item. If your profit on that $5 item is 100% of cost, you made $5, but if your profit on an item you bought for $10,000 is also 100% of your initial investment, you pocket $10,000. Which would you prefer?

## No Santa Claus and No Free Lunches

I learned early in life that Santa Claus doesn't exist. Most of my success came from hard work and never allowing anyone else to derail my dreams or discourage me. You may wonder why am I writing this book. That is a perfectly legitimate and reasonable question. I did it because I have been richly blessed in my life, and I feel an obligation to share my experience and knowledge with others so they can be successful too. It serves as a way of giving something back for the blessings I have received. But that is a topic for a very different book.

My wish for you is that as you follow your dreams and as they become a reality, you will also give back to others as you have received. Experience has shown me there is much greater joy in giving than in receiving. Like many other people who have carved out their own success in life, I had to work my way to the top. It always troubled me greatly that so few people really have the opportunity to be all they could be. Or if they do have the opportunity, they think they don't.

No doubt, many people think themselves incapable of improving their life. Some fear the opinions of other people — especially friends or family. They would rather face their worst nightmare than the dreaded question: *"Who do you think you are?"*, perhaps thinking they don't deserve better. The important thing is: I was **never willing to accept an ordinary life of mediocrity**, and I hope you won't accept it either.

### Beware the Get-Rich-Quick Promoters

There are huge numbers of get rich quick books and programs being sold on TV, in bookstores, and elsewhere. They all share several common characteristics:

- They tend to require a significant, up-front investment, especially if they involve a seminar in a distant city. There is nothing wrong with educational materials that teach sound principles and well-founded methods, but many promoting their wares are more interested in lining their own pockets with your cash than in helping you attain a better life.

I know several people who went to the bank and borrowed thousands of dollars so they could attend seminars on how to get rich. Huge numbers of people invest in books and tapes on how to turn their debt into wealth. But then they discover they were talked into a false hope. They are stuck with the debt they incurred for the seminar or the books and tapes, on top of the debt they originally were trying to get rid of in the first place! Common sense says these programs can't work.

- They often involve investing in risky deals. They may tell you that little up-front cash is needed. In the end you discover you didn't have to put up a lot of cash, but you are on the hook for a lot of money you now owe on a deal gone bad.

You can avoid a lot of risk by making sure you are in nearly complete control of the business environment you are working in. You cannot control the economy or what is going on in the world, but you can control what you do with your time and resources. If you buy an item at a good price and sell it at a profit, but at a price the buyer considers worthwhile, you are performing a valid service in the free enterprise economy. It is when you are not honest with others in order to make a profit that you lose legitimacy.

And speaking of control, if you are employed by someone else, consider carefully: What degree of control do you have over your income and working conditions? For most people, it's not much. Should you consider doing something about it?

Perhaps you are already happy with the way you are living now and don't want to have to change to a different career, relocate, or otherwise disrupt your life and the life-style you enjoy. But if you would enjoy having additional financial means at your disposal, then this plan is for you, if you understand it.

## Step-By-Step:
## Your Pathway to Financial Independence

The difference between my plan and those get rich quick programs, and what makes it unique is that it only requires that you repeat each step in the plan, over and over again, until you get the results you desire. If you only do that, you will be successful beyond what you now imagine, without overhauling your present life.

Any person can adopt and follow these principles of taking just one step at a time. It is so easy to understand. The discipline required for following these steps will be outlined later, and they will only take a very small portion of your time, usually in the evening hours or on weekends. Even then, it need not be a specifically scheduled time; rather, whenever you desire to work.

Just set aside a few moments during your day or evening. That's all you need for completing the program. It's up to you to decide where this time will come from. When the desire is great enough, most people can readily figure out a way to make time available to do it.

## Time: Your Most Important Investment

While the plan requires a relatively small portion of your time, how you spend this time and what you spend it on is of utmost importance to your success. Most of your research can be done at home, or during unoccupied spare moments at work, from books or the internet. For example, late evening when the family is in bed might be a productive time to spend an hour by yourself, doing some valuable research.

Your need for time to do a little research may produce another benefit: finding additional time to spend with your children doing homework or interacting with them. Husband and wife joining together on work around the house can be beneficial to the relationship as well. Many rewards come with spending more time with family, such as a closeness that may have been lost from being a couch potato. In fact, it is quite likely that the family will soon begin to show great interest in your new adventure as you start sharing it with them, and they could easily become your greatest supporters.

The time you use can be time you now are spending doing things that have nothing to do with your success or supporting your family's needs. Often those activities you participate in provide very little return on investment in them, and more often than not, they do very little to train your mind for the journey ahead in your life.

Most of this business — hunting for treasures — takes place on weekends. You can readily include your family in your treasure hunts and they will enjoy them as much as you do. My wife is always looking for bargains and Joshua loves to look at the trains and other toys as we go in search of treasure.

### Selecting Your Path to Follow

Antiques and collectibles were a natural choice for me because, as traveled, I found great enjoyment searching for them.  Also, these types of items fit into my plan especially well, because I love to live with them in my home. But the process is the same for every treasure hunter, regardless of what is used in their hunt.

The only question I needed to answer before embarking on my treasure hunt was *what types of items would I buy and sell*. The selection is unlimited. I knew I wanted my choice to be things that were beautiful and expensive. You may want things that have historic value or practical value, and that is perfectly acceptable.

I have always known that by buying low and selling high, it is possible to make a lot of money. I have found that a person who is a good salesperson is never out of work for very long. The reason for this is he or she makes the company a lot of money. My philosophy has always been why not sell for yourself and reap the benefits? You'll never get rich working for someone else.

I won't try to answer the question of what you should buy and sell, because it should be of your own choosing. On eBay alone there are over 50 million people buying and selling things each day. It shouldn't be too difficult for you to decide on something to sell that interests you.

You must figure out what interests you have and what your passions draw you to. These and other questions are important to think about, because the more interest you have in an item, the harder you'll work to buy and sell it, and the happier you will be with the results.

What you choose at first may change as your knowledge base grows. The more you hunt for treasures, the more things you'll find of interest. Maybe children's toys will be your first choice but later, you may realize your heart is in the collecting and selling of fine arts.

To my way of thinking, buying and selling things is the essence of a treasure hunt. Who wouldn't like to find a treasure? I read and re-read *Treasure Island* and watched the movie a number of times. I never tired of it. I was hooked because I would daydream that, someday, I would find my own special treasure; the one that was just for me that nobody else had ever found.

Over the last 45 years, I have found we all have the opportunity each day to find something that is meant only for us. There are more treasures out there than we will ever be able to collect, and certainly more than we have space for in our homes.

### Don't Sit On Your Assets

It is possible to collect and sit on too many treasures. That is why I have an agreement with my wife: I must sell something out of my collection each time I bring a new item into the house to keep. She made this rule because I have a painting hanging on every wall of our home, plus several vases adorning many of our tables. I have accomplished enough that it is now just as much fun to buy something to adorn my home with, as it is to sell a piece for a great amount of money. But, I now have an imposed limit on what I can keep.

You may find, as I do, that even if you have a beautiful antique in your home for only a short time, it will still bring you great pleasure while it is in your possession. Another wonderful thing about selling treasures to others is that you know where the treasures will remain, should you ever want to admire them again at a later date.

I am thankful my wife is so much more practical than I am. She continues to keep me on track to reach the goals I have set in this business: being financially independent. Likewise, for you we are talking about buying right and getting the most out of each piece we sell. While you will eventually want to keep some things for you own enjoyment, this book is about helping you first become financially independent. Once you reach that objective, you will then be able to keep the things you want, whenever you choose.

*French Clock*

# Part II

## Real Stories of Real Treasure Hunters
## in the Real World of
## Antiques, Collectibles, and
## Fine Works of Art

Many of my friends have used the principles in this book to their own substantial advantage. To illustrate those principles, I will show what they did and how they did it, by allowing me to tell you about some of their experiences.

# Chapter 3

## Real Tales of Real Treasure

### There Is No Substitute for Competence

My friend, Cecil, is one of the smartest people I have had the privilege to know in all my years in the antique business. I have learned a lot from him, and probably the most important thing he taught me was to continue in my pursuit of learning about the rare pieces that are out in plain view, just waiting to be found. As I traveled with him at times, I was amazed at his ability to pull a treasure out of a pile of junk.

Cecil and I have been friends for over 20 years. While browsing in an antique mall with him one afternoon, I watched as his eyes were drawn to a group of drinking glasses perched

*Kentucky Derby Glasses*

on a shelf. I'm sure you have seen them in your searches — maybe 20 or 25 glasses all sitting together. Most of the time there isn't one of them that is worth twenty-five cents, but this time was different. There was one particular glass with the design of a horse's head on its side. Cecil knew he had to own it. You see, he had done his research and studied those items that were rare.

The dealer was asking $13 for the glass but was willing to offer Cecil a 10% discount, making the price of the glass about $12, with tax.

The fact that Cecil attempted to negotiate the price of the glass with the seller is another important clue to successful treasure buying.

Never buy anything without asking for a discount. Everything is negotiable. If the price you offer is denied by the seller you can still purchase the item at the price originally asked. However, you must make certain that it still meets the standards you have established for buying your items. These standards will be outlined later.

> **>> Clue 5**
>
> Never buy anything without asking for a discount. Everything is negotiable. If the price you offer is denied by the seller you can still purchase the item at the original price. However, you must make certain that it still meets the standards you have established for buying your items.

To this day, I still wonder how nervous Cecil was as he left the store, knowing that he had just made himself a lot of money. You never want to celebrate until you are safely home with your treasure, because the sellers could be offended if you made them aware they had made a horrible mistake in pricing the item.

## Competence Pays Off

Two weeks after buying this very special drinking glass, Cecil sold it for $12,500. This particular item just happened to be an extremely rare 1940 Kentucky Derby glass, one of very few produced that year. How many people had held this glass and just passed it by?

So I ask you, did he find a treasure? He certainly did. But he also knew a rare item when he saw one. There are probably several hundred more glasses out there just waiting to be found, and one could have your name on it.

## A 2,000,000% Return on Investment?

If you watch the *Antique Road Show* on television, you may have seen the table that was purchased for $25 by a woman at a yard sale. The table was priced at $35, but she only had $25 with her, so she offered that, and the seller accepted. At the time, her purpose in buying was to fill a space in her home — a small table for displaying some of her trinkets. After having the table in her home for quite some time, she noticed a paper label on the bottom. Upon researching the name, she found it might have some antique value.

Although I don't know why she decided to take the table to the *Antique Road Show*, she had it appraised on TV, not expecting it to raise any eyebrows. There were many people in line, and she just continued to move forward. As she was waiting her turn, one of the brothers on the show asked if she would bring the table to where he could examine it closely. She quickly agreed, and they took the table to a private area. To her surprise, the appraiser asked if he could interview her on live television. On camera, they told her that, at auction, the table could bring as much as $250,000. She made the decision to consign the table later, and it sold for over $500,000! It is a life-changing event when a $25 investment suddenly mushrooms to a half million dollars.

I wish I could have taken a picture of her expression as the appraiser told her what he thought the table was worth. And that would have been nothing compared to the feeling that must have coursed through her as the table sold for over $500,000. There is little doubt she is now making a regular practice of stopping at all the garage sales, looking for another table just like the one she bought and sold.

I have heard lottery winners remark that even though they may have won one lottery, they never stop buying tickets. Even after that first big win, they know treasures can still be found. After all, they are living proof of it. I have heard of people who have won several lotteries, even when most of us think that winning one is impossible.

**<u>Note:</u>**

Winning multiple lotteries is not impossible, but lotteries are not an effective means for becoming wealthy. Many lotteries claim to return half of their total revenues back in prize money. That means if you spent millions of dollars buying every lottery ticket in a given "game" for a given period of time, *the best you could possibly expect* to get back by winning every prize would be to *get half of your money back.* Your odds are better than that just playing the slots in Las Vegas or Reno.

And as you look at the dazzling lights in those cities, always remember those fancy facilities are paid for with the money people didn't win, but left behind on their way out of town.

In this book, you will learn methods for becoming wealthy that are based on sound principles, using odds that you control, not odds set by others who want to fatten their own pocketbook at your expense.

## Comfort in a Comforter

Later, on another episode of the *Antique Road Show*, there was an appraisal of a Native American Indian blanket that was currently being used by the owners as a comforter. You could tell that the man who had brought the blanket wasn't expecting the appraisal to be over a few hundred dollars. This was a man who had worked hard all his life and never expected to strike it rich. I am sure that he was thinking, "I'd bet they don't even know the dog has slept on it!"

The appraiser from the show asked the owner of the Indian blanket if there had ever been anyone with great wealth in his family. He answered quietly, "No." To which the appraiser responded, "Well, there is now."

These folks brought the blanket to be appraised, and were told the value was probably over $300,000. I am sure he thought he must be dreaming.

It seems to me there should always be a doctor nearby when an appraiser informs people they have become wealthy simply by owning something they never dreamed had any worth. The doctor might be needed should their heart be unable to handle the shock.

I am sure the blanket was soon sold. Perhaps at even a higher value than the appraisal that was given. It would be interesting to know how much the blanket sold for, but even at $300,000 it would have been a tremendous amount for a couch comforter.

The woman who discovered the rare table and the people who owned the Native American Indian blanket are ordinary folks, just like you and me. They, like many others, are finding treasures every day. So why not you, too?

## More Tales of Treasure

Allow me to tell you a few more stories about other treasure hunters, including myself, who have also located items one could classify as treasures. These tales of treasure are useful studies in the art of treasure hunting, and are very instructive as you begin your study in mastering the art of treasure hunting. I hope you are beginning to see yourself in some of these stories.

### Treasure Ignored on the Bargain Table

Attending many estate sales, I often bump into the same people. There is a woman I often see at most of the estate auctions, and on one occasion, she told me an interesting story from her experiences.

On one of her many excursions searching for treasure, she entered an antique mall and walked it from end to end but found no success in her search. As she was leaving the mall, she noticed a bargain table. On it was an unusual candlestick, priced at about $70. After carefully examining it and finding the price appealing, she purchased the piece and stored it away, along with her other purchases of the day.

The candlestick was marked *Jarvie*, a very famous metalworks company here in the United States. The candlestick had been on that same table for a long time and was probably viewed by hundreds of people as they passed by. There it sat, waiting to be found by someone who recognized it as a "bargain".

After purchasing the candlestick, my fellow treasure hunter listed it for sale at a famous auction house that specialized in Arts and Crafts items. The candlestick was soon sold for more than $7,000.

Remember the name *Jarvie* as you peruse items sitting on bargain tables. You have now added this name to your growing list of things to watch for in your search. What may look like an ugly duckling, may in fact be a diamond in the rough.

This story brings to mind another important thing for you to remember. I'll reveal it in the next chapter. Happy hunting!

*Vintage Toys*

# Chapter 4

## <u>Thoroughness</u>

## <u>and the Art of Treasure Hunting</u>

Try never to pre-judge where your next treasure might appear. Don't leave from where you are searching until there is no other place left there to look.

Many treasures will be found among what seems like only trash, in places you would never have expected to find anything of value. I have found some of my best buys in basements, attics and garages. Always look on every shelf, in every box, and in every room when you are at a sale.

> **>> Clue 6**
>
> Try never to pre-judge where your next treasure might appear. Don't leave from where you are searching until there is no other place left there to look.

## Keep Digging

Make it a point to ask the person conducting the sale if you have missed anything of importance. By asking, I have often been led to something I missed earlier that proved to be one of my best buys of the day.

Here is my method of operation when I am shopping a sale:

- For my first pass, I make a sweep through the house, picking up those items I know I want to purchase. I carry them with me as I continue to look over all that is offered for sale in the rest of the house.

- The second time through, I spend more time, looking carefully, and giving each item my full attention. If I've overlooked something of value during my first pass through the sale, I can catch it this time.

- The third time through, I am just looking to determine if I have made any mistakes, or overlooked something that might be a great buy.

- Then, and only then, after I have convinced myself there are no other pieces of interest, I find a corner where I can take a few minutes to examine each object I have selected. I then return those things I have decided are not worth the investment or are damaged and of no interest to me.

- When I have completed my search of the sale, I proceed to the cashier to purchase all of my new-found treasures.

Soon I will list these items for sale, either on eBay, or at an auction, and wait for the results. This is a very exciting time because you don't know what the purchases will bring.

## The Early Bird Doesn't Get *Every* Worm

Now, on we go to the next stop on our day's shopping trip. Who knows what you might find just around the next corner.

You should realize that, as the day passes and you continue to visit sales, a lot of people will have already looked over the things that are still available, and fewer great pieces will still be available to you as time passes. However, never assume, just because other treasure hunters have gone through an estate sale or garage sale before you got there, that there won't be a treasure or two left for you.

## 150,000% Return in Seven Days?

I strongly suggest you take advantage of every opportunity to locate your treasure, regardless of where it might be. I have found that I am not smart enough to know where that next special piece will be located.

For example, I was on a family outing with my wife and Joshua for Father's Day. We enjoyed a day together that turned into a great story.

My wife had planned a trip to Lake Geneva for brunch and a boat trip to celebrate Father's Day. She asked me what else I would like to do on my special day. I told her I would enjoy stopping at any garage sales we saw along the way.

Though I was having very little success finding any treasures at the few sales we had visited, three-year-old Joshua was having a wonderful time looking at all the toys as we stopped along the way.

We were almost to Lake Geneva when I asked Vickie to stop at one more sale. Reluctantly, she agreed, and we climbed out of the car one more time.

At this sale we found a sleeping bag for a very reasonable price, but there didn't seem to be anything else of interest for me. As my wife was paying for the sleeping bag, I began to browse through a stack of dinner plates on a table. The fifth plate in the stack caught my eye, and, to tell you the truth, I don't know why. I suspect that after we have looked at so many things in our search, the subconscious mind simply interrupts our thoughts and tells us when we see something of value. This particular plate was about six inches in diameter and dark blue in color. There was a circle of white flowers around the outside, and on the top was written "My Plate." On the bottom of the plate it read "Dorothy."

It wasn't until I turned the plate over that I became really interested. In black script were the initials SEG. I knew SEG stood for Saturday Evening Girls and was made by a wonderful pottery company by the name of Paul Revere.

I approached the woman holding the sale and asked how much she wanted for the plate. She said she would take twenty-five cents. From the look in her eye, I concluded that she thought it was a fair price.

At the time, I didn't know the value of this plate, but I was confident that, for a quarter, it had to be a bargain.

I quickly paid the woman the twenty-five cents and stored my treasure in the car. The rest of the way to Lake Geneva Vickie kept asking why on earth I bought that plate. Obviously she had already concluded it would just be one of those things I had hanging around the house that we would never be able to sell.

When I arrived home that night, I went straight to my computer and listed the plate on eBay with a reserve of five dollars, thinking perhaps I might find a collector willing to pay that much for it.

After watching television for a while that evening, I decided to retire to bed, but first I wanted to check eBay to see if I had any bids on my plate. I wasn't expecting any bids in such a short time, but to my surprise, there were already three bids, and the price was up to $103. Wow! What a surprise! And I still had over 6 days left on the auction.

After seven days, the auction finished and the final bid

was an amazing $375. Not a bad return on a twenty-five cent investment. If you can do this with a quarter, imagine what you'd have if you spent $200 and got the same return. (The correct answer is $300,000).

### The "Print" that Wasn't a Print

There are so many stories I would like to tell you about people I have known and the treasures they have found, but space will only allow me to tell you a few more. I think you will enjoy this one about my friend, Jimmy.

I often see Jimmy at most of the estate sales and auctions around Chicago, which we both attend regularly. At one particular sale, Jimmy also found something that might be rightfully classified as a treasure. He was attending a local auction and spotted a framed painting which happened to be a small watercolor, hanging very high on the wall. The fact that the picture was hanging so high would suggest to most people that it was a print, but Jimmy had to verify it, just to make sure.

Jimmy is a true professional when it comes to judging value. I have often witnessed him working at an auction, and he leaves no stone unturned in his search. I've noticed that when his eyes land on objects of great value — often ones that have been overlooked by others — he examines them, but says nothing to the others around him about what he has found. He just places the item back where he found it, and proceeds to continue looking, acting as if it is of no value to him.

It is quite evident from Jimmy's lifestyle that he definitely knows his markets and has profited nicely from his fantastic results. As you travel, looking for sales to attend, you will often hear people talking about many of Jim's great finds. Many think of him as the person who possesses the greatest amount of knowledge in many aspects of this business around the Chicago area. He has become known as somewhat of a guru, and people follow him around as he previews a sale.

This result is what gives Jimmy the advantage when it comes to buying a valuable object. People seek him out for counsel, and he willingly shares his knowledge as long as it doesn't interfere with his quest. This knowledge you are now acquiring, hard-won by others, will, in the future, lead people to search you out. Your reputation as an expert in the field you have chosen will grow far and wide. You will find that people will want to partner up with you, which will lead to many great opportunities coming your way.

After examining the painting, Jimmy concluded it was done by a very prominent painter, Jessie Wilcox Smith. The purchase price for this painting was $45, which made Jimmy extremely happy. So happy in fact, that he couldn't wait to get the Smith painting home so he could do a further search on the history of the piece in the many books on paintings that he owns.

Jimmy had taken advantage of the rest of us by going that extra step of climbing up a ladder and closely examining the painting to verify that it was a watercolor and not a print. How many others, just as I, were a mere few feet from a wonderful find, but failed to go that extra mile and lost out in our search?

> ## >> Clue 7
>
> There is danger in over-confidence. We need to always be learning from others and not be too proud of our own knowledge. Nobody can know everything about this business, and you never know when a little piece of information or knowledge you encounter may pay off with tens of thousands of dollars, so it's worthwhile to keep your mind and your heart open.

There is danger in over-confidence. We need to always be learning from others and not be too proud of our own knowledge. Nobody can know everything about this business, and you never know when a little piece of information or knowledge you encounter may pay off with tens of thousands of dollars, so it's worthwhile to keep your mind and your heart open.

This incident is a good example of how I broke one of my own rules: I carelessly assumed the piece was a print without examining it. How can you ever know for certain what something really is unless you get your hands on it and examine it to verify whether it is "the Real McCoy", or something of lesser value? This also provides an opportunity to see if there is any damage that would decrease its value. You can now see how my carelessness, or more accurately, my own laziness, allowed me to skip going to the trouble to get the ladder as Jimmy had, causing me to miss an excellent opportunity to cash another large check. There went another treasure.

After discovering his prized Smith painting, Jimmy placed it in a local art auction in our area. You won't believe the hammered purchase price: $22,000! The auction house where he sold it was less than twenty miles from where he originally purchased the painting, but the results were certainly different. This proves you should never go along with the crowd, but rather, always do your own research before dismissing any piece as worthless.

### A Masterpiece Masquerading as Junk

This next story is also uniquely interesting. It clearly demonstrates how outcomes from your decisions sometimes don't turn out the way you expected.

Jim is a young man who lives in Florida. He was raised by his stepfather, who happened to be very interested in art, and often took Jim to museums so he could see the best art ever painted. Jim had even traveled to several countries in Europe to view the world's greatest art works by the most famous painters in history. Because of this exposure to fine art, Jim started to restore paintings as a hobby so he could bring worthless art back to its original beauty. He also began to build a rather extensive art collection of his own. The rooms in Jim's home were filled with old frames and paintings just waiting for him to apply his skills to them and make them worthy of hanging on someone else's wall. This is just a hobby for him, so many of the pieces he buys wait a very long time before he applies his skill to them.

Standing in an antique mall one day, Jim was approached by an elderly woman who asked him if he would be interested in buying a painting she had for sale. After examining it, he told her it was of no interest to him because he had more than enough old paintings to practice on.

He studied the painting again, but it was so dark from age and grime that it was impossible to even determine what the subject matter of the painting was, much less whether it would be of any value when restored. The woman insisted, asking only $25 for the painting. Because she was asking such a meager sum for the painting, Jim finally consented to buy it. He reasoned that if this lady later found something of greater quality and value, she might also bring that to him for purchase, and this was great advertising on his behalf for a very minimal investment.

>> **Clue 8**

Always be thinking ahead about what effect your dealings will have on the people you buy from or sell to. Make sure you treat them so well they will want to do business with you again.

Hidden in this story is yet another important clue, a learning moment, and a great lesson: You should always be thinking ahead about what effect your dealings will have on the people you buy from or sell to. Make sure you treat them so well they will want to do business with you again.

### Discarded and Forgotten, A Phoenix Rises from the Ashes

Jim took the painting home, placed it in a pile of old junk frames, and promptly forgot about it — for several years. One day, searching for an old junk canvas with a nice frame he could use, he came across the old painting. For some reason, he put a cleaning cloth to the canvas and began to clean it. He had no intention of selling the painting, so this was going to be nothing more than a little time spent, simply experimenting with different cleaning techniques.

To tell you the truth, the main reason Jim pulled this piece out of the pile was because he thought the frame would fit another painting he was working on. As he began to carefully wash away the dirt and grime, he noticed the most beautiful colors he had ever seen. The colors were so vibrant that he immediately recognized this painting could be of some value.

He soon discovered his experience and know-how were far from sufficient for him to properly restore the painting to a presentable condition, so he did what I will always instruct you to do. He called a major auction house in New York and asked for their advice. They told him to send the painting to a qualified professional who could clean it properly and perform any other needed repairs. They also provided him with the name of a competent restorer who could do the job. By using this restorer, the auction house could then confidently offer the painting to their clientele at auction when the work was completed.

> **>> Clue 7**
>
> This is Clue Number 7 repeated in a different context and in different words. It is *important*!
>
> Always be willing to ask for help if it is needed. In this business, it is impossible to know everything, and you will find that people are willing to help if you just ask.

This is Clue Number Seven repeated in a different context and in different words. It is *important*!

Always be willing to ask for help if it is needed. In this business, it is impossible to know everything, and you will find that people are willing to help if you just ask.

Are you ready for this? The painting was done by an artist by the name of Heade, and was called "Hummingbirds and Orchids." It was later sold for over $600,000 dollars at the same auction house where he got the advice. I'd bet he is now unusually glad this piece was not discarded, because it easily could have been.

An experience such as this could change your life very quickly, wouldn't you say? Every person will begin to collect their own stories to tell as he or she starts buying and selling treasures, and this is part of the fun we receive from this business.

### Smile for the Camera

This brings to mind yet another story about a young man named Warner, who has become my very close friend. A gentleman called me to look over some items he was offering for sale. However, after visiting his office and seeing nothing of interest to me, I called my friend, Warner, and suggested he might want to also take a look at some of these items. He didn't find anything he thought was of much interest either, with the exception of some camera equipment in the corner. He asked the man if it, too, was for sale. At the time, he had no knowledge of camera equipment, but this group of things caught his eye.

> **>> Clue 9**
>
> Never leave where you are before asking to look at anything else the sellers might be interested in selling, or if they know of someone who might have things to sell.

The clues for your success in hunting for treasures and building your fortune keep coming, and the lesson here is that you never leave where you are before asking to look at anything else the sellers might be interested in selling, or if they know of someone who might have things to sell. In this case, it was simply asking if items were for sale that didn't have a price tag on them.

The camera and equipment did appear to look somewhat different than most, so Warner asked the seller how much he wanted for the lot. He told Warner he would take $900 for all the equipment that was sitting there. Warner then called me to ask what I thought. I told him I thought he was crazy, but if he believed the camera and equipment were worth something, to go ahead and buy it but offer him $750. The gentleman quickly accepted our offer, and we began to hope that we had made the correct decision.

The camera turned out to be a Deardorff camera, made in Chicago during the early 1900's, and generally regarded as the Rolls Royce of studio cameras. I have to give Warner a pat on the back for having such a great eye for value.

Who would ever have thought it might have any great value? Another treasure nobody seemed to want, so it was passed over.

After returning home, Warner did some research and learned that the camera probably was a great buy. We couldn't wait to find out. The next day he returned to the sale and they gave him all the accessories at no charge!

As our excitement grew, we planned how we would list these pieces on eBay. We decided to list each item separately, hoping to double our money as we waited for that first bid. I am glad nobody offered us that amount, because I think we would have accepted their offer.

We didn't have to wait long, because on that first day the bidding reached $3500 for the camera — a bid far above our goal — and we still had six days until the sale ended. The final tally came to $5400 for the camera, and $1000 for the attachments.

This is just another example of how one should never pass up a chance to find a treasure. Every once in a while you must let your best judgment be good enough in making your final decision.

### From Customer to Partner

The story about how Warner and I met is also of interest. He was originally a customer of mine, visiting my home regularly in search of things to sell on eBay. He bought some Disney collectibles I had for sale, then, after they were sold on eBay and he had a little money, he called me again, looking for other items to sell. Next, I sold him some Royal Doulton figurines which he listed and sold in short order.

I began to realize Warner was very aggressive in his buying and selling, and I liked that. I invited him to be my

partner in hunting for treasures and we continued together in this business for about five years. I am confident
he would say these were definitely rewarding years, as do
I. Due to his other commitments and family needs, he had
to reduce the time he spent working in our antique business, but he started a new business on his own called the
*[Charles] Lotton Glass Collectors Club (www.lottonglassclub.*
*com)*. Now Warner is one of the most knowledgeable people dealing in that wonderful
glass, and he is recognized
by all the leading auction
houses in the country.

*Charles, John and Daniel Lotton Vases*

By the way, I personally
think Lotton Glass will be
the next Tiffany. Every piece
of the beautiful glass is
hand-blown and the crafts-
manship is outstanding. To
become the next Tiffany,
there must be enough pieces
that come to market for a
person to build a collection,
and in this case, Charles
Lotton has been producing
these wonderful pieces since
the 1970's, yet the value in
this wonderful glass is just
starting to be appreciated in the marketplace.

Warner and I are still the best of friends, and we talk
almost every day. Being in this business can lead to some
of your best friendships which then become a constant
source of information for both of you. I enjoy sharing with
the people I have met along my journey, because they can
appreciate my love for this business and the things we get
the opportunity to deal in.

### From $16,000 to $110,000 in Six Months

As I have stated before, knowledge is a precious thing,

and by doing just a little research, a treasure can be found. You may be wondering where I found some of my treasures, so I will expose you to a few stories of discovery.

In 2000, I bought a painting for $16,000 created by Frederick Morgan, a well known British artist. At the time I bought the painting, the highest price paid for any of his works was $280,000, so I was sure I had found a treasure. There was no way this painting could be worth less than $40,000.

I had only owned the piece for a short time when another work by Frederick Morgan sold a Christie's for almost $1,000,000. It was a little larger than mine and had a few more characters in it, but I think mine had more appeal.

The painting I bought was of two little girls jumping rope, and they were dressed in turn of the century clothing. I couldn't believe my good fortune because nothing had ever happened to me like that before. My painting was auctioned six months later for over $110,000 at Christie's in New York.

The interesting thing about this painting was that many people had looked at it before I had a chance to see it. In fact, as the dealer was showing it to me, he said it was on hold for someone else. The dealer who owned this painting had to have made a profit on it, so what do you think he paid for it? But on with the story.

The clues never stop, and here is another one: There is a lot of talk in this business, but you must always be as good as your word and ready to take action.

> **>> Clue 10**
>
> There is a lot of talk in this business, but you must always be as good as your word and ready to take action.

I did my research, then called the dealer, requesting an opportunity to buy the painting if the other sale didn't go through. Two weeks later he called and told me it was available if I was still interested. I bought it, then — like any normal person — began to wonder if I had done the right thing. But in my heart, I knew I had.

Never give up if you think you have found a treasure, even if you may have a little doubt at the time. By now you should be beginning to see that the opportunities are endless, and your confidence will continue to grow as the dollars, likewise, get larger and larger. The stories that I am sharing with you now will soon be your own.

### Don't Give Up When Down on the List

I was attending a conducted sale and the woman in charge told me there was a great Newcomb vase available. When I inquired about the price, she told me the asking price was $5,000, and I immediately said I would take it. When I asked where to pay, she told me I'd have to get a number, which would have been 68. This meant I would be person number 68 in line to see it, and, with every dealer in Chicago there for the sale, it was obvious my chances of buying it were going to be very slim, so I went home.

Later in the day, I returned to the sale, and much to my surprise, the vase was still there. The lady came running up to me and asked if I still wanted the vase. I confirmed that I was indeed still interested, but not at their asking price, because everyone else in town had seen the vase, and obviously they didn't think the item was worth $5,000. She asked if I wanted to make an offer, so I looked around to see if there were any other pieces I might want to purchase. I found four pieces I thought would bring over $2,000. Not wanting to tip my hand, I offered $3,000 for the vase.

The offer was quickly declined. I was told the owners would not accept that amount, but they would be willing to entertain another offer. Playing it very coyly, I made them wait a few minutes while I looked around some more. I then told her I would give $3,200 for the vase and the other four pieces. By then it was late in the day and most things at the sale were sold early that morning. I calculated that I might have a decent chance at that price. She came back and informed me I had made a purchase.

Earlier, I would have willingly paid $5,000 for the vase and $1,000 for the other four pieces for a total of $6,000, but now I owned them all for $3,200.

I sold the Newcomb vase in Cincinnati, Ohio for $13,500, and the buyer got a bargain. The other pieces sold for close to the $2,000 I had originally estimated. I am very glad I returned to the sale, even though I didn't think I had a chance of being able to buy anything.

### Let Others Be Your Eyes

As you can see, there are many opportunities to make a lot of money in many different kinds of Antiques and Collectibles. Your stories in the future may come from old interests you had as a child, such as coins, stamps or sports cards — or perhaps new things you may want to venture into.

To give you an example of what I mean, I became very interested in Western Art because of the many trips out west my family took. I began looking for paintings by artists who painted near where we vacationed, and I discovered the work of a Wyoming artist appealed to me greatly.

My wife and I usually spend at least a week at the Eaton's Ranch in Sheridan, Wyoming each year. Once, while in Sheridan, I visited the local galleries and found paintings by a local artist, who signed his work, "William Gollings." His work had great appeal to me, but I never thought I would ever own one.

Your search for treasure will help you develop personal preferences, and this is when it will really start to get exciting for you. Returning home after a few visits to the ranch, I put out the word that I would like to find a painting by this artist. To my surprise, a friend in California called and told me he had found what I was looking for.

This painting was a wonderful discovery of Mr. Gollings' early work from 1904. It showed ten cowboys riding in a trail line as they were approaching the observer. Given that it was a small painting — about six inches by fourteen inches, but very well done and with fabulous colors, I knew it was a great value when I bought it. The price was $12,500, which I was more than glad to pay. Later as my collection grew, I decided to sell the Gollings, and at auction it brought nearly $30,000 at the Treadway Galleries in Chicago.

That is much better than money in the bank don't you think? If you are looking for special items, be sure to have everyone you know be on the lookout for you, and they may come your way from very unexpected places. As I have stated before, items can come your way by simply passing out a card or telling someone on the phone about items that you are searching for. I told a friend, Bob Higgins at Higgins Maxwell Galleries, that I was interested in Kentucky art. Since that conversation, Bob has brought me over a dozen paintings which I have purchased from him.

### How To Mug A Big Fish

In terms of percentage return on my initial investment, one of the most profitable purchases I ever made was a Royal Doulton mug. I had collected Royal Doulton for quite some time, and had established a reputation in our area as one of the most knowledgeable people on the subject. Even though my collection of figurines and Doulton Lambeth would match most of the important collections to be found, I never had much interest in the mugs. However, I always keep my eye out for the special mugs by Doulton.

One day, my wife was in Atlanta doing an audit for her firm, so I decided to go out and see if I could find something to buy. After spending most of the day unproductively searching the places where I usually expected to find bargains, it was time to try a different area. The North Shore area of Chicago had always been good to me and seemed like a sensible place to go to spend the rest of the day.

Most of the shops I visited had few items of interest and my watch warned that closing time was fast approaching, but there was still time for one more look in a little shop not far away. Immediately after entering the front door, I spotted a Royal Doulton mug and picked it up to check the condition and the information on the bottom. As I examined the specimen, the owner who had been standing in the corner approached me and asked if I was interested in the mug. Before I could even respond to his question, he told me he could only discount 10% off the asking price, which seems to be the standard discount for most dealers. That percentage is supposed to make you feel like you are getting a bargain, even though they usually are willing to take off much more than that if you only ask.

At the discounted price of $165, prudence insisted that I purchase the piece, so I bought it immediately without seeking any further discount. Suddenly the day was like a fishing trip where I was getting ready to pull up anchor and head for shore. But there was still one more important cast left in me that I must make. I now had the bait that would produce the biggest fish of the day.

Fishermen are notorious for telling tales about "the big one that got away," but I was bubbling from excitement because that last cast landed me a very big one that didn't get away. Arriving home with that next prize, I could hardly stand the wait for the call from my wife in Atlanta. Finally the phone rang and the first question she asked was what had I done all day. I told her I spent the day antiquing, and of course she had to ask if I had bought anything. Relishing an opportunity to tantalize, I responded blandly, "Yes — A Royal Doulton mug."

Her attack was immediate: "You better not have. We don't even collect those." Her next words set her up for the kill: "What did you pay for it?" she asked.

Now it was my turn at the bat. I calmly responded, "I paid $165." Then I paused a moment before continuing — "but one hour ago I sold it to a dealer in Miami for $6,500."

The silence on the other end of the phone must have

lasted two minutes before I heard her say, "Do you have the money?"

## There's No Substitute for Knowing Your Stuff

You must be asking how could this have happened when the mug was in a antique shop owned by a well-known dealer. After all, he had done his homework and gone to the *Ruth Pollard Price Guide of Royal Doulton* to look up the price. If you looked up that piece today, you would see that the guide even shows a picture of the piece. The name of the mug is "Arry", and the number is D 6207. The price that he had quoted was $185, just like the dealer's price guide shows.

One of the most important skills you need to master in order to maximize the best opportunities you will encounter is to know the rare, not the common, items you are searching for. The dealer knew the right place to look, but he didn't take the trouble to discover the correct price on this mug. Had he gone further into the guide, he would have found another listing with the same picture and the same number D 6207, but with a very important difference. The name: *Pearly Boy.*

The only difference between the two pieces is the decoration. The Pearly Boy has pearl buttons on its collar and a row of them on the hat he wears. Both pieces in the guide came out of the same mold, but value often depends greatly on the decoration. The guide priced the large Blue Pearly Boy, which is the one that I bought, at $7,500 to $9,000. I got a wonderful price for the mug, but I am sure the dealer did quite well too, because he must have had a customer waiting for an opportunity to purchase this rare piece from him.

Stories like this can be yours. You will have even more than I if you master the principles. I hope by now you are beginning to catch the fever, but there is so much more that I must share with you before you start your journey. I have told you this several times already, but I want to be sure that you remember to always be looking for the rare instead of common items. The story of Pearly Boy demonstrates this principle.

I could tell many more of these stories of finding treasure, but I think it is time to set you out on your own treasure hunt, in search of your financial independence. Once you set your goals, there isn't any place to go but up, if you master the principles I present. I am well along on my journey. The Frederick Morgan painting is my greatest treasure so far but now I am looking for that million dollar find.

*Hutshenreuther - Short Haired Pointer*

# Chapter 5
## Preparing for the Journey Ahead

Are you ready to begin this adventure? If you are on board and ready there are things to know before we start to explore the method that you will use to make all your dreams come true. I must first tell you the basis for this book, which will give you a better understanding of the principles you will be using for the rest of your life.

You must have a plan before you can start your journey. If you don't know where you're going, how will you know when you get there? None of your plans will turn out exactly as you expected, because life is full of pitfalls along the way. But you need a plan to give you direction and to use when measuring your progress toward your desired end result.

No plan is worth its salt if it can't be implemented and end with a successful conclusion. The government makes you file a business plan with them before they will extend a Small Business Loan to you. Likewise, the bank wants a business plan when you apply for a loan. So why shouldn't you have a workable work plan to follow when you are going to enrich your life to the maximum?

> ## >> Clue 11
>
> You must have a plan before you can start your journey. If you don't know where you're going, how will you know when you get there? None of your plans will turn out exactly as you expected because life is full of pitfalls along the way. But you need a plan to give you direction and to measure your progress toward your desired end result.

### Let Us Suppose...

There is a principle most wealthy people understand very well that you need to know about. To illustrate, let's suppose you and I are participating in a television game show called *Who Wants To Be Rich?* I am the host and you are the contestant who has just beaten the odds and all other players. You are now in place to get the Grand Prize! No doubt, many people who are interested in the kind of treasure-seeking venture we are embarking on would jump at an opportunity to win cash on a TV show, even if it wasn't for a lot of money. And some of them are probably watching us right now.

To maintain the suspense for you as well as the national audience, your prize is located in one of two beautiful boxes, each sitting on a dazzlingly decorated pedestal. You will now have to select Box Number One, or Box Number Two. But this show is different. Before you select the box you want, you will be told what is inside each box.

First, I must clarify the rules of the game: Once I tell you what is in each box, you will have only five seconds to make your choice. If you fail to make a choice within that time, you lose, and get nothing! Can you feel the pressure? I announce, "Door Number One contains a check for *One*

*Million Dollars tax-free!"* The audience is wild with excitement.

Of course, we all know that nothing in life ever comes easily. We hear all the time that there is no free lunch. But people still sit, glued to their TV's, watching somebody else make a pile of money, yet they seem to enjoy it. Could it be they are living the experience vicariously? In reality, are they not putting themselves up there in the contestant's seat?

When I disclose that Box Number Two contains one single, solitary, very ordinary copper penny, the audience sits in stunned silence. As I talk about it being a very ordinary penny, murmurings of disbelief begin to filter softly through the studio air. The penny in the box is not a rare coin or a collector's coin. It is only a very common penny like you see every time you pay for groceries and the clerk opens the cash drawer. Obviously the audience is wondering if it's a game show stunt.

But there is a catch. I explain that you get to take the penny home as your first payment for today. Then tomorrow you will receive another payment for two cents, four cents on the third day, and so forth, doubling in amount every day until you get paid the last doubled payment on the thirty-first day. After the thirty-first day, you are paid in full with nothing more coming, forever.

You have five seconds. Make your choice, starting... *right...now.*

So what did you choose?

I am emphasizing these simple concepts and principles because they form the basis from which your great success will come in the future. I wish I could make this more complicated, but I can't because it simply isn't.

If you fully understand the next few paragraphs, your life will be changed forever. Many, if not most people today wouldn't even bend over to pick up a penny if they saw one lying on the street. However, after reading this book, you will be looking to find that copper cent every day. Now back to our game show.

Your time is up. It's time to select your prize. It is a choice that can completely change the direction of your life's pursuit. Both options will make you financially secure for at least a time, but one of them will have you exuberantly screaming for joy knowing that the sky is the limit. Have you made your choice?

If you are like most people, you would have taken the million dollars — a sure thing — and no one would have faulted you for that decision. You would be quite glad to get it, and you would have just become this country's next millionaire. But I hope I have dangled enough clues so that you would guess by now that choosing the million dollars would have been the wrong choice to make. But if you were like most people, and had taken the Million Dollars, it would be time for me to give you the unfortunate news you thought was impossible: You just made a very bad decision. It may seem hard to believe, but here is the proof:

| Day | Pay | Total | Day | Pay | Total |
|-----|-----|-------|-----|-----|-------|
| 1 | $0.01 | $ 0.01 | 9 | $2.56 | $ 5.11 |
| 2 | $0.02 | $ 0.03 | 10 | $5.12 | $10.23 |
| 3 | $0.04 | $ 0.07 | 11 | $10.24 | $20.47 |
| 4 | $0.08 | $ 0.15 | 12 | $20.48 | $40.95 |
| 5 | $0.16 | $ 0.31 | 13 | $40.96 | $81.91 |
| 6 | $0.32 | $ 0.63 | 14 | $81.92 | $163.83 |
| 7 | $0.64 | $ 1.27 | 15 | $163.84 | $327.67 |
| 8 | $1.28 | $ 2.55 | 16 | $327.68 | $655.35 |

Let's face it. The first week (days 1-7) weren't very interesting. The next seven days not much better either. Days 15 and 16 are getting a bit more interesting. Let's continue. Rounding the cents up to the next dollar for day 16 to calculate day 17, let's take a look at the rest of the first 30 days:

| Day | Pay | Total | Day | Pay | Total |
|---|---|---|---|---|---|
| 17 | $ 656 | $ 1,311 | 24 | $ 83,968 | $ 167,935 |
| 18 | $ 1,312 | $ 2,623 | 25 | $ 167,936 | $ 337,581 |
| 19 | $ 2,624 | $ 5,247 | 26 | $ 337,582 | $ 671,744 |
| 20 | $ 5,248 | $ 10,495 | 27 | $ 671,744 | $ 1,343,487 |
| 21 | $ 10,496 | $ 20,991 | 28 | $ 1,343,488 | $ 2,686,975 |
| 22 | $ 20,992 | $ 41,983 | 29 | $ 2,686,976 | $ 5,373,951 |
| 23 | $ 41,984 | $ 83,967 | 30 | $ 5,373,952 | $ 10,747,903 |

## Putting the Icing on the Cake

By now, you can't wait for the arrival of Day 31! That check will be for over $10.7 million, making your total take for the 31 days nearly 21.5 million dollars! That's a whole lot more than the other option of "only" a cool million.

This principle is called **compounding**, and you will never look at pennies the same way again, once you understand its power. But you don't have to be a "winner" on some imaginary TV game show. You can take this knowledge of compounding, apply it to some principles of buying and selling in a way that can double your funds on each successive transaction until you attain the same result in your own life. All under your own control, without being under the thumb of somebody else.

I will soon be telling you how it is possible for you to take these 31 Steps of compounding for yourself. When you do, you will become the captain of your own ship. The bank, who used to be your financial partner because you owed them money, will become your money manager. Or, if they work hard enough for you, perhaps even your financial advisor, as the money begins to accumulate in your bank account. Gone forever will be the day when they were able to regulate your life because now they borrow from you so they can lend to others. You will be carefully examining their financial position instead of them looking into in your credit report.

This simple little game-show story will be the basis for

your success — the foundation of the plan you will develop to fulfill all of your dreams. Now you have discovered the meaning of the title of this book– *31 Steps to You Millions in Antiques & Collectibles.*

## Which Is Best?

When I tell people the million dollars versus a penny story, most tell me they are going to go out and get their first penny, then start doubling. My hope is that most people would pick up their first penny and start moving ahead. Doing this would redirect the course of their life. By doing this and not continuing their present course, their hard work and mental effort would greatly enhance the quality of their life and they can still enjoy the rewards of their present job. By doing this you will gain financially from your hard work and dedication and soon, the income from your job may become the minimal part of your income.

> **>> Clue 12**
>
> Unless you see yourself successful, you won't be successful. You will never get to the top of the mountain until you climb that first step. *You will never become all you can be by always taking the safest route.*

The fruit of your labor should always first benefit you, but this is not to say you shouldn't do your best at the workplace, even if you believe that you are not truly getting paid at your job what you justly deserve. Rest assured that by following this program, this will soon matter little in your life. You can spend your whole life working for an hourly wage or a salary, but I guarantee that you will never achieve the wealth or success that I envision for you.

## It's Your Life. Take Control of It.

Pay attention to this clue: Unless you see yourself successful, you won't be successful. You will never get to the top of the mountain until you climb that first step. To climb this mountain you will need knowledge and equipment. That is what I will be assisting you with. You will never become all you can be by always taking the safest route.

Compounding is a wonderful concept but it is rarely taught in the schools today. Our children and students are taught the basic skills like arithmetic, reading and science but many of the common sense applications never see the light of day. Skills, like how to balance your bank account, how to change a flat tire and how to plan a simple trip are usually something you have to learn from a friend or mentor. As your friend, I guess I'll be the one to teach you about compounding.

It's up to you to use all of your talents and skills to secure a bright future for yourself, free to enjoy the joy and pleasures of life. By understanding and using compounding to your own advantage, you can start saying, "I am marching to the tune of my own drummer. I am creating the means and have the ability to make my own choices," if you so desire.

> >> **Clue 13**
>
> ***Compounding*** is the key to accumulating wealth, and you will find that most great fortunes have been made using this principle in one form or another. There is no faster way of meeting the financial goals you plan for yourself than to compound the money you have set aside for your future.

On the other hand, if you are one of those especially fortunate souls who really enjoys what you are currently doing, you can keep doing it, but put yourself in a position where money is not the object driving what you do. Then, if you desire, you could even do it without pay. Or if you prefer to keep receiving compensation, you would have an external resource to live on, should you come to a time when it makes sense to go in a different direction, yet have no concerns about finances when you make the change. It's called *true financial freedom*.

Here is a great clue for you to remember: *Compounding* is the key to accumulating wealth, and you will find that most great fortunes have been made using this principle in one form or another. There is no faster way of meeting the financial goals you plan for yourself than to compound the money you have set aside for your future. Compounding is simply doubling what you have, time and time again. The faster you can do this, the sooner you reach your goals.

The wonderful news is: If you can continue to double your money, it doesn't matter what you started with, because in a short time, you will be amazed at what you have accumulated and what power this gives you over your life. You will be able to do what you want, when you want to do it, no longer having to ask someone else's permission before acting in your own best interest.

## Invest So Your Money Helps *You*

What does our society teach us about money? When you have earned it, put it in the bank, right? We have all struggled to save those few pennies that didn't go toward the bills so that we could receive a small percentage interest on it in our savings account. By doing this our money might double in seven years if we are lucky. That's not at all bad. In fact, it's a far better return than most people get on their investments, including stocks, bonds, and mutual funds.

But what if you were able to do double your money every six months or even every thirty days? As I help you develop your plan, you will see that, if you let your money work for you rather than relying exclusively on investing your time on a job, the results will be astonishing.

By now, you're probably wondering, how can I double my money so often with out taking a great risk? This is what I will be showing you as we continue. In fact you will be learning how to double your money in this way with very little or no risk, and you can control the risk yourself instead of being at the mercy of the economy or other factors you cannot control. Does that appeal to you? Then keep reading.

## Keep Your Success and Direction

To succeed in the very big way I am recommending, start with this rule and never venture from it: *COMPOUND, COMPOUND,* and *COMPOUND* again. I hope you have that word permanently etched in your mind.

*This is the second time I have brought this to your attention because it is doubly important.*

Significant money may come to you very quickly because of the compounding effects from your activities, but *your eyes must stay on the long-range goal.* No matter how much money you've made, unless the goal you have set is reached, you must *Never, Never, Never* touch the money in your bank account. Not to pay bills, not to buy a car — not even to purchase a house, even if you can do it with cash. It is to be used exclusively for buying and selling treasures.

The goal is the challenge. Until it is reached, you have not fully succeeded. Only *31 STEPS* of compounding and you will be wealthy beyond your wildest dreams. And it is definitely worth waiting for, even if you have to drive that old car a little longer or live in your present house a few years more. Why risk staying where you are, because you blew your seed capital, when, by just waiting a little longer, you will be able to live on your *interest income alone*!

The instant gratification you will receive by owning that new car or house will soon fade away, but for your long term well being, if you wait for these things, the wait will be well worth it. Each step you take, when completed, will make you feel like a giant and give you a great amount of pride in your achievement. This growth in self esteem will be something you haven't experienced since you scored

> **>> Clue 14**
>
> *COMPOUND, COMPOUND,* and *COMPOUND* again. I hope that you have that word permanently etched in your mind. Only *31 STEPS* of compounding and you will be wealthy beyond your wildest dreams.
>
> This is the second time I have brought this to your attention because it is doubly important.

that touchdown in school or were chosen as a cheerleader for the team.

It sounds so simple, and it is. That is why most people can't accept it. In 1957, Richard Knerr and Arthur "Spud" Melin took a piece of hose and a wooden peg, then connected the ends of the hard plastic hose with the peg, forming a circle. The hula hoop was an instant rage. The company they founded nine years earlier — Wham-O — became a household word, and millions of dollars went streaming into their bank accounts. A year later, they topped that with a flying disk they called *Frisbee*.

So simple. So why can't we all do it? Don't allow yourself to be the one they are talking about when they ask, "Why didn't someone else do it?"

## Start Small — Grow Fast

This plan, based on compounding, assumes you are going to start with a very small investment that will not affect your present income or savings. Your risk will be almost non-existent. This money will be used to buy objects that are to be sold for at least twice what you paid for them. The money from the sale is then used to purchase the next object or objects which are then sold for twice that amount, and so forth. This is what compounding is all about.

The way you manage the money you start with, and the discipline you show while spending it, will enable you to reach all of the goals you have to set for yourself then consistently work toward. Your learning and understanding will also go straight up, much like your bank account, which will follow a similar path. Others will be amazed by your new found financial savvy and will come to you and ask for your help. The top of the mountain waits for you, and your eyes are only looking upward. This plan is based on the 31 Steps mentioned before, combined with your dedicated effort to complete them.

I suggest your initial goal should be to complete at least

one step in your journey every six months. You may be asking, "What will I do with the rest of my time?" The answer is, do the same things you are doing now. If you follow your plan for only five years with an initial investment of $100, your total will be over *$100,000.*

Now for the really exciting news: With that one-hundred dollar investment plus five years, if you continue for two more years, you will be near the Two-Million-Dollar mark! Now think: Why should you stop now when the sky is the limit? If you remember the stories, Cecil would have completed his first ten steps in two weeks on that one transaction involving the Kentucky Derby Glass, so it doesn't have to take six months for each step. That is up to you and your buying skills.

If you could complete ten steps each year for three years, you would be a multi-millionaire. The more money you have, the easier it is. I will explain that in later chapters, but first I must be sure you understand what we are working with and why it is so powerful.

You must be feeling, "I want to go and find my first buy," but wait. I have more to teach you about the proper ways to buy. After you have completed this book you will have plenty of time to shop for those special pieces. But first, we must provide you with some tools you will need for competing in the market place, then it will be buy-sell, buy-sell, and watch the money grow.

Be aware. This is not a game with me, and I take this business very seriously. As I share it with you, if you can't see yourself at the mountain top, it is best to not even begin, because it will only lead to disappointment for you.

I am on the lookout for people who want to excel and be that special person like the ones mentioned in this book. I am here to help you, but only if you want to help yourself. What you say won't be as important to me as what you do. Always remember: Actions speak louder than words.

## Detours Have Consequences

I started a young man out on this program and he was the best pupil I have ever taught. He was a natural. Everything he bought seemed to sell at the highest prices he could have imagined. The money just kept increasing. But one day he saw a used Mercedes he just had to have, so he bought it. He came to me later, after several days had passed, and asked if I would help him start again, but he had broken our cardinal rule. I wished him the best. The last time I heard from him, he was trying to make it as a starving artist.

Dreams only come true if you are willing to stay the course. I can't set your goals for you, but I can help you reach them if you are committed to finishing the race.

## Where Do I Start?

By now you are asking, "How much money would be needed to be successful with this plan?" What you start with is really unimportant, because if you remember the illustration, it was done with a penny. I would suggest you open a special bank account for your business with one hundred dollars in it. This gives you the opportunity to buy more than one item if you prefer. Besides, most banks now require an initial deposit of $100 to open a new account. Note that it does not have to be a business account. Many banks offer free personal accounts but charge for a business account. On the checks, you can have printed your name then "Special Account" or "Collectibles Account" on the next line before your address.

After starting your account, pick a name such as "Yesterdays Antiques" or whatever you think is a great name for your new company. You can then put this name on your business cards. To save money, you might get pre-perforated business card stock at an office-supply store, and print your cards, ten per sheet, using a computer and a good printer so you get good print quality. You are now in business, and the sky is the limit.

But what do you buy? This is strictly up to you, because this plan works with anything you are interested in buying and selling. I suggest making it something you enjoy being around, because you are committed to spending time and effort making sure your company becomes successful.

It is wise to take some time and carefully consider your decision on what kinds of items you want to trade in. I like to remember that old saying, expensive things can come in small packages, so I chose things I could easily carry and ship. If you are still ready to proceed, let's get started.

*Patty Prather Thum (1853 - 1926)*

# Part III:
## Strategies for Buying

## Chapter 6
### Buying: The Rules of the Game

You've heard the old saying: "Don't work *hard*, work *smart*." The trouble is, most people who say that don't know how to work smart. If they did, their lives would be much different. Successful buying must be centered on how you think. As you learn to think right, you will also learn how to buy right.

Before you can learn to think right about buying, you need to know the rules for buying. The nearly universal first question I am always asked is, "How do I know I can sell what I buy?" This is an alert, showing me I have a lot of teaching to do, because they are just barely starting out the door, and they're already worried about the wrong things. One could say, they are on the wrong end of the dog, or they have the cart before the horse. I will be explaining what's wrong with this later when we discuss the art of buying, but first I want you to study and learn this very important, fundamental lesson:

> **>> Clue 15**
>
> *If you buy right, you will never have to worry about selling whatever you have bought because the collectors will be lined up at your door to buy your items from you.* Always take your time in buying, and make sure you aren't buying just to be buying because this will become a fatal mistake on your journey toward success.

Now it is time to give you the secret to buying: *If you buy right, you will never have to worry about selling whatever you have bought because the collectors will be lined up at your door to buy your items from you.* Always take your time in buying, and make sure you aren't buying just to be buying because this will become a fatal mistake on your journey toward success.

Time is on your side, so sit back and relax. There have been treasures waiting to be discovered since time began. Just think of the oil in the ground. It has been there for a very long time. Perhaps even millions of years, waiting to be discovered by someone who had a dream of finding a gusher.

### Cushion Yourself Against Falls

Don't buy everything because it might look good. We are looking for the exceptional, not the good. Your time is valuable. If the profit isn't worth your effort, then you should pass it by. I use the "25% Rule." I try to buy each item for 25% or less of what I think the retail price for the item would be.

This gives me plenty of room for errors I might have

made in my judgment, plus it keeps me from buying everything I see that might interest me. If I am able to buy items that meet this standard of the 25% Rule, then I have enough wiggle room to negotiate with while being reasonably certain I can at least double my money. *Doubling is your friend. Never forget it.*

It is not uncommon that the items you buy will often bring much more than just twice what you paid for them. Remember my previous stories of great windfalls, where many steps were completed in one swift trade. The biggest mistake most dealers make today is they think they must buy *everything* that will make them money. What a mistake this is. Dealers often work on ten to twenty percent profit margins, which almost guarantees they will fail in the antique business.

The margins have to be great enough so that if you make a mistake, you will still be protected. At 10%, there is no room for error, which means you will soon be out of business. Also, if your margins are too small, ordinary business expenses will quickly eat up your profits. You will be left with items you can't sell, and again, you are out of business.

### Stay Away From Common Stuff

I met a lady recently at an estate sale, and we talked about the past. About five years ago, I took her under my wing and tried to show her how to be successful in the antique business. Here she was, five years later, telling me it was time for her to try something else.

Why was this? First, she was still looking for $5 and $10 items to sell. I could tell she had worked herself to death with very little to show for her effort. Second, I had warned her many years earlier: If you only buy common things, your inventory will consume the money you have, and this will limit your buying power. As a result, the steps you are trying to complete in your climb to the 31st Step will be halted before you get started.

## Keep Your Money Busy Compounding

It is critical that you make sure there is money in your account for those special objects that come along, and that you don't have all of your money invested in items where the inventory can't be sold in a reasonable amount of time. If this happens, you become like the "tar baby", stuck to your old inventory, with no money for the treasures waiting for you just around the corner.

If you are able to consistently buy pieces at 25% of their retail value, you have the luxury of being able to take some time in trying to sell them near their retail price. If this doesn't work after an appropriate period of time, you can then wholesale them at 50% off of the retail price, and still reach your goal of doubling your money.

Let's run the numbers. If you buy an item for 25% of its retail value, then sell it for 50% (half) of that retail value, you have doubled your money and completed the first step toward your millions. Simple enough? Then take all the money from that sale, go buy another piece. Then, again, sell it for twice what you paid for it, to complete another step.

This gives you double or more in return on your money every time you buy and sell an item. It really is that simple. I find it hard to figure out why we don't see everyone doing it. It certainly is simple, but it is not always easy, mainly because some people are unwilling to educate themselves into a different way of thinking.

But what a great feeling! And it doesn't matter whether it was ten dollars or a thousand. Every time you double your money on a transaction, you can beat your chest and feel like *King Kong*. In fact, those first steps as you start your climb, may well make your adrenalin flow more than the later steps where much more money is involved. Maybe it is because, later, you know the plan works. After all, you've already completed some steps. And you've become more accustomed to it.

## Highest Use of Your Dollars

Now let's look at what you've done financially. You doubled your money in a short time. Imagine taking the amount you used to buy the item, and putting it in a bank passbook savings account at 3% interest. With compound interest, it would take about *24 years* to double in amount, while inflation erodes its buying power to about one-fourth of what you started with over that same time interval. So which makes more sense: To tie up your money for decades and to let the bank make money on its value, or put it to work in your own business and double it every six months or less, rather than four times per *century* at the bank!? You stay well ahead of inflation at that rate when you wisely invest. This is a no-brainer.

You absolutely have the right to feel successful when you make that first purchase and sale. You'll feel it like you've never felt it in your life. It's a feeling nothing else can give you. You will feel like a financial giant, and you have that right. You've earned it. Money is coming into your bank account and it is growing ten times or twenty or a hundred times faster than if you had just put it in the bank to collect interest. You've heard bankers and other "experts" say, "It takes money to make money." Guess what. They don't know what they're talking about, and you just proved it. Let your business grow while funding itself. You'll never need to borrow a dime for the rest of your life, once you get the process well underway. Instead of the bank wondering when you're going to pay them, you'll be checking their credentials and financial disclosures to make sure your money is safe in their bank.

## But What Do I Buy?

You are unstoppable now. Everyone you meet is hearing how wonderful this business is, and you are getting free advertising at the same time. You'll never take out a loan to fund your business. I ask you, what could be better than that? The money is there, and you are willing to buy again. But what do you buy? As I said before, I will leave that up to you because I want it to stay fun and exciting for you.

There are millions of things to buy. I personally don't deal with furniture because of the size and weight. I don't want to be a mover for someone else, plus I am just too old for that kind of activity. Also, you have to own a truck or rent one, and there must be another person to help you move the furniture. There goes part of your future profit, even before the furniture is sold! However, furniture can be a great source of income if you don't mind the labor and trouble of shipping. However, you must have a place to store it until it's sold.

As with any collectible, if you select furniture for your plan, it is always wise to know and understand the trends in furniture before you buy. Modern pieces from the 1950's and 1960's are in fashion now, and can provide great returns on your dollars. People in their forties and fifties grew up with this furniture, so they are buying it to relive the life they had with their parents.

Furniture from the 1920's and 1930's is out of fashion. You will find it very difficult to make the percentage profit on furniture from this period that will meet our goal of doubling our investment, because there are fewer and fewer people who remember it from their childhood.

If you choose furniture, you may want to try finding Early-American pieces such as Quaker, or hand made pieces from the east coast or deep south. These pieces have become real antiques and their value reflects it. They will provide the profit you are looking for, if they have been bought properly, using our rules for buying. *Remember: twenty-five percent of the retail value.*

I find it much easier to handle items I can ship by mail — things sometimes smaller than a bread box — so these are the areas I have chosen: pottery, glass, porcelain, silver, toys, figurines, guns, knives, advertising, paintings, dolls — and this is just the beginning of my list. Stop by a book store and skim through the many references on the shelves under collectibles and you are sure to find things that will hold your interest.

### Use Reference Guides to Make Your Job Easier

Believe me when I say it is easy to find objects that interest you. Resources to help you determine their value can be found everywhere if you just take the time to look. There are great books in the library and most bookstores. You will find these references vital for making good buys. They also include price guides on almost any item you may want to pursue, so be sure to use them to the fullest. Here are just a few: *Rookwood Pottery* by Herbert Peck, *Carnival Glass* by Bill Edwards, *The Beer Stein Book* by Gary Kirsner and Jim Gruhl, *Roseville Pottery* by Sharon and Bob Huxford, *Depression Glass* by Gene Florence, and there are many more. These guides will give you much more than just a price. They include histories, references, descriptions, and over all trends for the objects they cover.

Several companies produce an assortment of price guides for various areas of interest. The most popular guides are produced by *Kovels, Warmans,* and *Schroeders,* and they are important companions to accompany the reference books. Always be aware that these guides are based on retail prices from the accumulated sales at major auction houses and other experts' opinions. Since the guides reflect retail value, never forget that you must buy at not more than about 25% of the value stated in most guides. There are books on every kind of collectible and antique you can imagine, plus some you never would have thought of. Another good source is through your computer and the internet, where the information is freely available, and almost unlimited. I have found I could spend as many hours as I wanted, just researching on the internet.

Sometimes I spend many hours just scanning the internet to see what kinds of things are popular today. To my surprise, I often see pieces I have passed up. By researching, I am able to discover my oversight, return to the places where I have seen them, and, if they are still there, add them to my inventory.

## Don't Be Afraid to Make Mistakes

As you gain and expand your knowledge, you will find it easier to use your efforts wisely in your pursuit of your goal. You'll be ready to step out and start your search. The beginning of this search is easy. All you have to do is to take the time, and have the desire plus a few dollars in the bank.

As you start out, you need to be brave and aggressive. Don't fear making a mistake. You don't have enough knowledge or enough money in the bank to make any really big ones. Your starting buys and sells are for only five, ten, or maybe twenty dollars. You aren't trying to buy a painting for $80,000 yet.

So you see, you can only make small mistakes at this point. If you make one, it won't destroy you personally, and it won't do major financial damage either. So relax, and enjoy looking forward to overcoming the inevitable errors on your way up.

Beware, though. I am not suggesting you go out and do anything really dumb, thinking you'll still make it. As you gain experience, you will learn how to identify the items you can buy and sell at a good profit, as well as what items you should not buy because the profit potential simply isn't there.

Just be willing to try and fail on a small scale so you can gain the skills you need while learning the business. Then, later, you can really "connect" on those pitches that you can completely knock out of the park. These are the skills that make ball players famous, and these are the skills that will make you very wealthy as you ascend the 31 Steps to your millions.

Being brave and aggressive at this stage helps build your confidence in your ability to judge the items you are purchasing. It will also help you learn to act very quickly on your best judgment when the occasion calls for quick, accurate judgment and immediate action, like when I bought and sold the Pearly Boy mug for a very healthy profit in mere hours.

## Mistakes: A Prerequisite to Success

Most people are afraid they will make a mistake, so they let their fear stop them in their tracks. Set aside any fears you may feel. You have plenty of time to research your item before you buy. Read and study as much as might be necessary, and evaluate everything that comes your way. Through study and observation, you can develop the skills that help eliminate the kind of errors others may fear.

We can ease and overcome our own fears by acknowledging the truth that every person makes mistakes from time to time. Mistakes are part of the human condition and a necessary part of our mortal experience. I am often reminded of all of the failures and defeats Abraham Lincoln suffered before he became one of the *greatest* Presidents this country has ever known. If you study his life's history, you'll see that he started from a very humble beginning. Most people thought he would never amount to much, but history has proved them very wrong. He never gave up on his dreams, regardless of what others thought or said.

Like Lincoln, you will also have critics. Maybe only a few, perhaps many. But you *will* have them. One key to your progress will depend on your willingness to not take counsel from them. You are the captain of your own ship. The master of your own destiny. You were created with the power to make choices in your life. Pursue and achieve noble desires, then put them to good use in making life better for those around you.

Obviously we don't want to make careless mistakes, or continue to make past mistakes. The ability to limit those errors is a critical key to being successful. The failures we encounter will test us, it is certain. But our accomplishments will be judged by our successes, not our failures. Don't dwell on your mistakes. They are only temporary set backs — stepping stones to accomplishment — that will soon be overcome with your next purchase.

Wisdom isn't achieved by success, but is a result of over-coming failures. We must continue learning. You will be amazed at the knowledge you can gain by just spending a few hours each week studying different price guides, reference books, auction catalogs, and the internet. You should continue to do this as long as you are in the business. The knowledge gained will stay with you as the hunt begins. You will be able to draw on this knowledge whenever you need it.

The information you retain comes in layers. First you might learn about Roseville pottery, followed next by perhaps Weller. As you start to absorb this information into your memory and your understanding, you will find yourself becoming very well informed on many different things. As a consequence, your chances of finding something of interest and value grows tremendously.

Remember, once you have stored this information and understanding in your mind, it can be called upon at any time. Other people will be astonished that you don't have to consult other means to identify or price the items you find. Your mind will be able to search out the necessary details from your memory as they are needed.

The ability to draw upon your own memory also saves you a great amount of time when you are buying or considering an item for purchase, because you don't have to look up each item as you examine it. This is one of the great advantages this plan gives you over other buyers, because, now, people will be coming to you for information. This will give you opportunities to buy from them.

>> **Clue 16**

Most dealers study the common items because they feel safe with them. They only buy the common merchandise so it can be turned for a quick profit. By doing this they can only make a small percentage profit on their investment– not double their money. And remember, our goal is to double our money. The *real* money is to be found in rare items.

## Repeat: Avoid the Common Stuff

Here is a clue that can give you a great advantage over others: Most dealers study the common items because they feel safe with them. They only buy the common merchandise so it can be turned for a quick profit. By doing this they can only make a small percentage profit on their investment– not double their money. And remember, our goal is to double our money. The *real* money is to be found in rare items, and you will hear me say this time and time again.

Buying cheap items is the wrong approach, as I have stated before, because you can find the value of these pieces in every mall, shop, auction house or antique show you visit. Your competitors will know as much about them as you do. The real money is not in the common items you see every day. It is in the rare ones that seldom appear, and that is why most people don't recognize them. If you know how to recognize, identify, and place a value on these items, you will have such an advantage over almost everyone else that it will seem almost unfair. You have heard the saying, "Knowledge is power." That was never more true than in this arena.

If you examine the stories in earlier chapters, you will clearly see how others passed by treasures because they were unable to recognize them as rare. So the items just sat there — waiting for someone with proper knowledge to come by and swoop them up. By identifying those rare pieces, you cut your competition down to nearly zero.

Dealers also shy away from expensive pieces because they are often afraid to take the risk, or they don't have the money to spare. They also don't trust their own judgment about the value of what they are looking at. I have found that when the price of an item is above $1,000, the competition for it is reduced tremendously. Ironically, that is also where the most profit can be found. Therefore I want you to concentrate here.

You want to be the *champion*, not the contender, in this

climb. Go where no other man has trod and where others still fear to tread, and what you are becoming will get you to the prize first.

## How to Avoid the Disadvantage of a Lean Purse

Never let a high price on an item be the determining factor in your decision to buy or not to buy. I have found pieces I couldn't afford, so I called a friend to see if he might be interested in splitting the cost and profit. On paintings, I have many people who have told me if I find a painting that is too expensive for me, they would buy it and split the profit between us. I have found this to be a very fair and equitable way to deal with people who don't have time to go searching for treasure but still have an interest in these wonderful objects. They put up the money, I do the work, and we split the net profit from the overall deal.

There is always a way to make a purchase if the piece is being bought correctly (buying correctly means when the piece is sold it will bring a full 100% profit or more on the initial investment). Remember this, and have it burned deep into your brain. This is the secret that will set you above the average dealer.

Also always remember: When you are trying to value an item for purchase, you must always use more than one determining factor in that decision. If you use a guidebook, never forget the book is just that — a guide. Guidebooks are nearly always out of date, and the true value of an item can be less, or very much more, than it is listed for in the book. Guidebook prices must be combined with many other factors whenever you set the value. One factor you might use, for example, is that you have just seen this piece sell on eBay for a price much unlike the guidebook price.

You will discover that items rarely sell at the prices listed in most guidebooks, but the guidebook does provide a starting point on which to begin the evaluation of an item.

In fact, you will usually do well to get half of the listed price, so always use as many resources as you can find on each item before you make an offer.

The history of auction prices will be our best guide to current prices for like items, and they will be the best guide to present values. Even then, you must be especially careful if you can only find one price listed for the item that sold at a particular listed price. This could mean two people got into a bidding war, and the winner overpaid for the piece. In such cases, you have to throw the sale price out of your calculation because it is an anomaly.

Whenever you evaluate a piece, always remember: You will find the suggested prices will vary tremendously, and you want to come to a fair and reasonable estimate for the items that are presented to you. So take your time in evaluating each piece.

*French Potty Vase*

# Chapter 7
## Buying: Where To Go

You have heard a lot of stories and also been given clues on how to buy, but where? Let us tackle that question and see where the answer leads.

Before we get bogged down in the details, always remember: You can buy anywhere you find objects available, but they must be at a price you are willing to pay, and

> ### >> Clue 17
>
> *You can buy anywhere* you find objects available, *but they must be at a price you are willing to pay,* and that price must always comply with the 25% Rule.

that price must always comply with the 25% Rule.

## Family, Friends, and Neighbors

*Family, friends, and neighbors* are always a great place to start buying. I suggest making a list of the kinds of things you would like to buy. Give a copy to everyone you know, and tell them you are starting a new business. Be sure to put your name, telephone number and e-mail address on the list. You will be surprised how many people will search you out to buy their belongings.

I have even had kids in the neighborhood stuff mail boxes with my list. The results have been amazing. It has since come to my attention that this constitutes tampering with the mails, and is illegal, so don't do it unless you want trouble with the postal inspectors. As an alternative, you can use printed door hangers instead, and have them hung on people's doors. I do suggest, for your own protection, that you contact local city authorities to make sure there are no prohibitions against the practice where you live. Usually you can find out the rules for your area from the police department or zoning officials. However you do it, be sure to keep it neat and be careful to prevent your information from blowing or falling off, or ending up as trash in their yards.

Another source I use is having flyers placed under windshield wipers on cars in malls parking lots, *but only after getting permission to do so from the mall management.* Failure to get permission could have you facing trespassing charges.

Community bulletin boards, restaurants and other public places can also be a great avenue for your postings. Your reputation and image to potential customers or sellers is very important to the success of your business, so make it a professional presentation.

Once people begin to find out about your new business, they will show great interest in what you are doing, and they will become your greatest helpers in finding the things you want to buy. These people will become pickers for you, and it doesn't hurt to reward them for their efforts. I usually give about a 10% finder's fee as a reward to the pickers who point me in the right direction to great treasure.

Word-of-mouth is the greatest advertising in the world, and soon people will be calling you saying, "Aunt Jane has some china for sale," or, "My friend wants to sell a painting. Would you be interested?" These people will begin to love helping you because they want to help you become successful.

Jewelry is one category I get a lot of calls on, and there is always a market for jewelry. This takes up very little space, and it has two values: The value of the material it is made of (gold, silver, diamonds, platinum), and value based on its design and eye appeal.

What a great business this is and no wonder it has been kept secret for so long by the ones who are making all the money from it!

*Remember: Never refuse to go and look at a single thing people have.* What you go to look at, and what you eventually buy from them may be two entirely different things. You may think you will only find junk, but someone might have given them something special that has value of which they are unaware.

One time, a woman asked me to come to her home to see if she had anything of interest to me. After I arrived, she began to tell me stories about where some of the things she had came from. For instance, her uncle once worked for a very prominent family in Chicago, and the family had given him two old lamp bases that had become tarnished, with rotted cords. She had inherited them, and her husband wanted to throw them away. But she decided to find out if they had any value.

I looked at them, told her they were Tiffany lamps, and offered her $3,500 for the pair. She gladly accepted. A few weeks later, I was able to sell the pair of lamp bases to a

Tiffany collector for close to $10,000. There are many valuable treasures hidden among much trash.

### Garage Sales

On the weekends there are always *garage sales* you can attend. You are just starting out in this business, so use your time wisely as you prepare for the sales. You will remember, I said this business wasn't going to change the things you were doing in your life. I scan every publication I can get my hands on that might help me in my search. Usually all of the estate and garage sales are listed in daily newspapers on Thursday. Chart the addresses on a map to plan the route you are going to take for the sales on Friday, Saturday and Sunday. Always keep it with you. Attending the sales can be completed in a couple of hours each day. Garage sales are especially good places to find things because the sellers aren't experts on the items they are selling.

When going to a garage sale, be sure to get there early. The professionals often get there before the sale starts, often at daybreak, so plan to be at the sale as early as possible. Don't waste time. You are there to look and buy. Do your business and go to your next location. If you see any friends at the sales, please tell them you will call them later, but right now, you are doing business. Most garage sales require cash, so be sure you have money with you.

People holding garage sales begin very early in the morning and their most valuable things are often in the house, so be sure to ask if everything that is to be sold is outside. Try to get ahead of the crowd. This may require starting at the back and working forward at the sale. The things being offered at these sales may be items they inherited or purchased many years before. I have told you values change, and if a person bought something twenty years ago, the current price could have increased ten-fold since then. A Tiffany lamp may have been bought in the 1950's for $5,000, but today it might bring $100,000 or more.

These sales are where you will see the most junk, but there are also treasures. I once attended a garage sale that was being conducted by a fifteen-year-old girl for her grandmother. I walked up and dropped my teeth. There were Miessen figurines, Daum Nancy glass vases, Royal Doulton, and many other quality things. I told the grandmother to stop the sale and I gave her an appraisal of what I thought the things she was selling were worth.

She stopped the sale, but I don't know what had been sold before I arrived. I am sure there were many dealers that day with smiles on their faces. The Grandmother told me she would call me later, and I could help sell the items I had picked out. But I never heard from her. I often wonder where those beautiful antique pieces ended up.

We aren't in this business to cheat someone, but to make an honest living. Always know that you will have to live with yourself after the money is made. I never want to wonder if there is someone looking for me because I took advantage of the situation they were in.

After you have attended the sales, you may want to call the numbers listed in your newspaper classified ads where people have individual items for sale. If you find things you might be interested in, there still might be time to go and investigate to see if they meet your guidelines for purchase.

If you are at a sale and find something you are interested in, don't set it back down until you are sure you don't want it. This holds true, no matter where you are, because the next person behind you might pick it up and it is gone.

You can also tell the person conducting the sale what you are looking for and they may lead you to the best pieces before others find them. If you are buying a large piece, most sales put colored dots on them to indicate they are sold. That way you can identify all the pieces you have bought without having to tote them around while looking at other items.

Always be polite, and be sure to leave your card. Ask if

they have anything else to sell, or when their next sale will be. By doing this, you might get a surprise in the future when they invite you to attend a pre-sale they are having. A pre-sale is when they let some of their preferred customers in before the sale begins, so they can select the items they want before the crowds arrive.

There have also been occasions when people asked me into the house where I found all kinds of things I was interested in. While others were outside looking through the ordinary items they had set out — things of no interest to me — I was inside, buying the best they had to offer.

### Flea Markets

On weekends, you may want to attend flea markets. Again, I advise you to get there early. I have seen buyers going up into dealers' trucks and vans even before they were unloaded, demonstrating that the merchandise is picked over fairly quickly. I was in Indiana at a flea market and before daylight, buyers were using flashlights and going into the trucks before they were even unpacked! The dealers looked as if they couldn't believe their eyes!

At this sale there was a hall tree I would have liked, but another dealer got there first, even before the sale started. I was very disappointed, not having a chance to purchase it. After this, I began my search and about an hour later, I saw that same hall tree in a booth with the price raised by $300. This was an all-day trip for me, so I stayed till the very last minute. As I was leaving I couldn't believe my eyes! There in another both was that same hall tree, and again, the price had been raised an additional $500! This definitely proved to me that my judgment was correct about that piece.

You might have this happen to you as it did to me: There have been several occasions when, after purchasing an item, I would be approached by another dealer asking if I wanted to sell it. I know I would have to ask for at least a 100% mark-up on it for profit to keep within my guidelines. I usually decide it is much better to keep the item and do my research. I might find out it is worth more than I ever expected.

It is very important to know how most flea markets are laid out because it will help you plan the pattern you follow as you canvas the sale. Most of the valuables will be found in the barns or other buildings on the grounds. I usually go there last because these dealers know their merchandise, and the only way to find the bargains you are looking for here is if they have made a rare mistake. For me, it is best to start at the outside vendors' booths. I have found some of my best buys in these areas.

I often go directly to the back of the lot and work forward because this gives me the first look at items that might meet my rules of buying, before the crowd works their way from the front to the back. Most of the dealers who set up outside are looking to turn their merchandise at the sale, to provide themselves with funds to spend on items for the next sale.

Most outside dealers are not professional antique merchants. They work the sales on weekends to create some additional income for themselves. I have found most of these dealers aren't very concerned about the true value of the pieces they have for sale. They are more interested in simply turning a profit for themselves. Make your first pass through the flea market fairly quickly. You can always go back later for a second look. Also, be sure to wear comfortable shoes when you attend these sales because you will be doing a lot of walking. The last thing you want are blisters cutting your shopping day short.

At these markets, there is always room for negotiation, so don't be afraid to make an offer that is far below the asking price. If you try to buy a piece but are turned down, you may want to go back to that dealer later in the day. If the item hasn't been sold, he may be more willing to sell it to you at your offering price. As I told you, I have on occasion actually bought a piece, then sold it to another dealer at the same flea market before I left for the day, but I only do this on items where I am sure of the value, so there is no need for further research. Of course it also meets my 100% rule. That certainly falls within our six-month rule for turning an item as we climb to the next step. As you can see, sometimes steps can be completed very quickly, and escalate your ascent to dealing the larger and more valuable pieces.

Be sure not to let the weather stop you in your search. When the weather is bad, the dealers are often more willing to deal, and there are fewer people to compete against. Your shopping may be more profitable on day like this.

Be sure to eat before you go so you can continue your search while others are stopping to eat. It also helps to carry some treats in your pocket just in case those old hunger pangs hit you. Also be sure to carry some water with you. A couple of bottles in a small pack attached to your belt can save you a trip to the water fountain while you're trying to make time. Just don't overdo it, or you may find yourself looking for a rest room more often than otherwise necessary. If the weather is hot, dehydration can be a dangerous enemy. Remember: This is like a race. Usually the first one out on the track, armed with the proper knowledge and resources in hand, gets the treasure.

At these markets, hand out your cards to everyone you meet, and be sure to list what you're looking for, along with your phone number, on the card. All upcoming Flea Markets in your area can be found in *AntiqueWeek, Antique Trader, Antiques and the Arts Weekly* and *Maine Antique Digest*.

### Antique Shows

**Antique shows** are my least favorite shopping venue. These, however, can be the best place to acquire knowledge about the things you are searching for. You can find experts here in every field willing to answer any questions you may have. Where else could you find so many people with this knowledge in one place, and not have to pay for the information they so readily provide?

After trying to place my great pieces at a retail price without success, these dealers have been a great resource for me when I sell my great pieces at wholesale to them. This is because these dealers have large customer accounts waiting to be called about some rare or unusual item that can be added to their collection. Often, the price doesn't matter to them. For this reason, if they can find those special items their customers are seeking, and buy them at wholesale prices, they can still make a lot of money on them.

Take the whole day at one of these shows, and you will accumulate more knowledge about the rarities we are looking for than you could in six months of reading about them on your own. The other advantage to you is that the pieces can be held and touched, so if you see similar pieces in a different location, you will recognize them easily.

Most shows feature a wide variety of fine antiques and collectibles for you to search through, but you will usually find the prices are too much to pay if you expect to reach your 100% goal. Just like at the Flea Markets, if you attend the first day and find several things of interest to you but they are too expensive, you may want to go back the last day near the close and see if those items are still there. If they are, you may learn that the dealer hasn't had a great show and may not have covered his expenses. He might be quite willing to work out a great deal. If that is the case, the dealer may agree to reduce the asking price by more than half, enabling you to purchase some genuine bargains.

The more shows you attend, the more dealers you will become acquainted with, you'll broaden your base of information and creating a wider market for future sales. Always be sure to exchange cards with all the dealers and let them know what you are looking for. And, of course, always keep your tool bag close to you, with all your tools in it. You never know when you will need it.

Sometimes dealers preparing for a show will find items that do not interest them for their show inventory. But, when they run across your card, they remember you listed those items as pieces you are interested in. Having your card provides an easy way for them to contact you. These dealers are able to conveniently dispose of the items, you get them at a good price, and you can turn them into a better profit. The dealers usually only charge you a commission for this service. In doing this, you have just added another pair of eyes to your search for the negligible cost of a business card.

Seldom will you find a bargain at the antique shows, but it does happen. The dealer may have found an item and brought it along, but it is not one in his area of expertise, so he prices it very modestly, like the dealer who had the Royal Doulton mug but didn't know the rare from the common in Doulton.

Usually there is an admission charge for going to shows, but it is well worth the ten to twenty dollars it takes to get in. I recommend that you attend as many antique shows as possible when you first start out. The information you will accumulate and the resources you will add to your list will be invaluable to you.

Don't be bashful at these shows. Pick up everything that catches your eye and check it out. This will give you a point of reference if you see another item like it in the future. Also ask questions, ask questions, and ask questions. Questions like: "Why is this so expensive?" "Were there many of these made?" "How can I tell a fake from the real thing?" I always ask the dealer if he or she has anything at home that I might be interested in. They may have a painting in their home that they would sell reasonably because their specialty is silver and they just picked the painting up thinking it was cheap. They might be willing to sell it to you at a bargain price. You never know until you ask.

These dealers at the shows are usually reaching out to the true collector or other dealers from other areas of the country. They will be taking their purchases to sell in their areas, such as on the east or west coast. Usually they are not going to be able to sell to us and allow for the profit margins that we need.

## Estate Sales

**Estate sales** can be one of your best places to buy quality goods. This is a sale where everything in the house is priced. The people conducting the sale usually let from ten to twenty people into the house at a time from numbers assigned before the doors are opened. If you have a higher number, you can expect most of the bargains will be gone by the time you get to enter the house to search for them. There are exceptions to that rule because I have found great pieces late in the day at these sales — such as the Newcomb vase I told you about earlier.

When advertising the sale, the house-sale company will set a time when you can get your number before the actual sale begins. If you rely on the published time, you will find it is usually too late. If you want to be one of the buyers who gets the bargains, be sure to be there early. A reasonable person would expect to show up, be near the front of the line, if early, and get a low number. However, there is a practice, common among dealers, that will put you much farther down the list of numbers issued. Here is how it works:

Suppose there are several house sales in an area, one at 9:30 A.M., another at 10:30, etc. Some dealers will send one of their people to each sale very early, perhaps even as early as 4:00 A.M. They will start a list of people, putting their buddies' names on the list first, even though they aren't even there, then perhaps adding to the list names of other people who arrived early.

At 8:30 A.M., when the sales company gets ready to issue numbers for the 9:30 A.M. sale, the dealer will give them the list and receive low numbers for their own people who haven't even arrived on the scene yet. This gives them a huge advantage in gaining early access to the best items. At sale time, several of them are in the first group to gain entry, and they pick up as many of the best items as they want or can, leaving everyone else to get the lesser quality items.

I wish estate sellers would refuse these lists and let people into the house based on their position in line as the sale starts. Unfortunately, the dealers are their largest customers, so any change in the future is unlikely. Common sense dictates that it would be fair to treat all the buyers at the sale equally and fairly. In all other sales where a rush of interest is expected, the general rule is always "first come, first served". Estate and house sales should be no different.

Believe it or not I have spent the night in a person's driveway when the sale was particularly interesting to me. This assured me a position first in line, and most of the interesting items I was searching for ended up in my box.

I have been training a young lady who had quite an experience when I asked her to do me a favor. A special house sale was scheduled at a time when I was going to be out of town on a ski trip, so I asked her to represent me. Of course she consented, but I don't think she understood that, to be first in line, she would have to be at the sale location at 2:30 in the morning, long before sunrise.

After I gave her my instructions and she got over the shock, I told her when she entered the house she was to just tell the person in charge that all the paintings are sold. She took a deep breath, then asked me how much she should pay for the paintings. She was even more baffled when I said, "Whatever they are listed at in the sale." I spent well over $10,000 at the sale that day, and I wasn't even there! I gave her a pat on the back, told her she had done a good job, and we are now partners.

The major problem with this type of sale is that when the door is opened, it is like a stampeding herd of cattle. Everyone is rushing around, and if you find something, you must pick it up and keep it with you or it will be gone. This type of buying gives you little time to think, so you must depend on your instincts. One thing you must do is use your time in the house to your best advantage. One way to do this is to look in through the windows from outdoors and try to map out where you will go first when your number is called.

At these sales you don't have time for talk, so if anyone tries to stop you and wants to chat, just tell them to catch you later. The first look on each item is usually also the last look you will have, so you must train your eyes so you can skim a table or room very quickly and spot the things that might be of interest to you. There are always several of these sales each weekend, so map your path to them so that your time is used at maximum efficiency.

Often the starting times will be different at these sales, so always take this into consideration when scheduling your visits. You may find it advantageous to visit several sales very early before their starting time so that you can be on as many lists as possible. Then start your search with the one that starts earliest.

When buying at these sales, it is okay to make a lower of-fer. Sometimes they are accepted, but most of the time they are rejected if you make the offer on the first day. Often, they will invite you to leave a bid and your phone number, promising to call you. I have been able to buy items this way on occasion, but some of the sellers use your bids to get someone else to pay more than your offer.

A better way to buy from these sales is to return the fol-lowing day. The sales companies usually reduce the prices on their items 50% on the second day, so you may be able to buy what you want at a price that makes more sense, provided, of course, that someone else didn't already buy what you were looking for.

### Internet

The **internet** has opened a whole new world of com-merce, and buying and selling collectibles has not been left behind. Access to many of the items you are interested in is unlimited. There are millions and millions of people now using the internet, making it the largest market on earth. I started to use the internet to access eBay shortly after eBay became available. It has proved to be my greatest tool in this business.

I use the internet every day to do research, and also to keep up with the auctions I have running on eBay. The great thing about the internet is that it doesn't matter whether you are buying or selling. Either way, there will always be people wanting to do business with you, day or night.

My friend, Cecil, taught me a lesson about eBay. He often lists the same item several times if it doesn't sell. The reason he does this is he knows different people will be seeing it each time. For example, he listed a piece of pottery and it didn't sell for the reserve price of $150. But after re-listing the same piece, it brought over $300, well worth the extra effort of relisting.

Some things you should know about when using the internet: When I am bidding for an item on the web, I always e-mail the person to see if they might have other things to sell that would be listed on eBay in the future. (Note that I am only looking for advance information about future items. I am not attempting in any way to divert business away from eBay. They provide a valuable service.) Also be sure to e-mail the seller about any questions that are not answered in the listing. If the seller has an eBay store, you should take time to look at the other items currently listed in the store.

People find the internet is a great way for disposing of things they want to sell, and this gives me a wonderful place to buy. I don't have to leave my house to do business, and the whole world is opened up to me.

I have bought items from individuals in almost every state in the United States as well as Japan, Australia, Germany, France and most of the Countries in South America. There is no way I could function in this business today without the computer and the internet. At first it seemed very dangerous, but with time, people using eBay started to get feedback (comments posted by people they have done business with on the internet). If these are positive, you can feel relatively sure that it is okay to deal with them. If there is no feedback or negative feedback, you must take appropriate precautions.

The way I usually handle potentially risky transactions is by using an intermediary to assist me on the transaction. I might have an auction house where the person lives take delivery of the item. If it is as described, I then send the money for the item to the auction house. The auction house then pays the dealer/person, and sends me the item. I pay the auction house a small stipend for their services.

Another precaution you can take is to ask if you can come by and pick the piece up and pay for it, or, if it isn't in your town, can a friend of yours pick it up for you. This will stop most people who are trying to scam you.

One may hear all kinds of horror stories about trades on the internet, but I can tell you that I have made several thousand trades with no major problem, so far. I have had damage in shipping, but I always insure the things I buy, and I have always been paid by the insuring company.

If you have doubts about the seller, have him call you and see how you can work with him so you will feel safe. Always be courteous to the seller because you may be doing additional business with him at a later time. The hope is that he will always be accommodating.

Be sure to leave positive feedback for all the people you have a successful transaction with. Upon the completion of each transaction, update your files with the information on the purchase or sale.

Once the seller receives your payment, it might be difficult to get your money returned if there is a dispute. It is always better to be safe, rather than sorry, when you are dealing with people where you have to have the merchandise shipped to you.

When you are considering bidding on an item, be sure you know what it is you are buying. This is your responsibility. If the seller listed it correctly but you didn't bother to read the description carefully, that's your problem. You should ask as many questions as it takes for you to feel comfortable that the item is what you wanted to purchase.

Internet auction sites always have a place on each listing to ask questions. Be sure to use it. There are also other places to buy on the internet besides eBay, such as Yahoo and several others. I use eBay the most. I have found them to be trustworthy and helpful. They also conduct live eBay Auctions that list things from other auction houses so you can bid on them live, as it happens.

In the 1990's, if someone had told me that I would soon be able to sit in my office and bid for antiques in a live auction, as if I were actually there, I would have said they were crazy. Welcome to the new world. This is a great resource for you to use for purchasing those items that interest you. Many of my best buys have come from these live auctions.

These live-via-internet auctions are usually listed one month in advance. That gives you plenty of time for research and questions. I once bought a Rozenburg plaque online at an auction in Florida for $1,000, and sold it to a Canadian for $5,000 the next day. Thank you internet. I could not have done this any other way.

There are many places on the internet where you can list what you are looking for, enabling millions of people to see your listings and respond if they are interested.

You can greatly limit your mistakes by reading very carefully. Always make sure the item is listed properly. Pay attention carefully to the words and phrases, such as: "Like Tiffany,", "looks like Daum," or other descriptions that tell you it's not the real thing; merely a reproduction with low market value.

Google is also a great place to find buys. All you have to do is go to the Google web site and type in the item you are looking for. You will get lists of links to more information than you ever would have dreamed possible. There will also be links to other web sites where you can buy and/or sell almost anything. Yahoo! and other internet search engines also provide similar capabilities. For example, typing *tiffany glass* into the Yahoo! search engine produces over 5 million links in mere seconds.

You can limit the number of links you get back from a search engine by being more specific in your search criteria or using the site's "advanced search" feature. This allows you to be very specific about what you want and what you don't want. Using search engines effectively enables you to access large amounts of information efficiently so you can become well-informed about the present market, and put yourself well ahead of most other people in the business.

Be careful when using search engines. Certain search criteria can return links to sites you may not want to access due to the nature of their content. If you want some degree of protection in this regard, there are filters that you can turn on in your browser that can block objectionable materials. Just be aware that some purveyors of such material are quite creative at appearing to be something very innocuous, but when the page appears on your screen it consists of inappropriate subject matter.

### Regular Auctions

I have found and bought most of my treasures at **regular auctions**. I have been attending auctions since I was young. I found myself mesmerized by the atmosphere I always encounter when attending these events. Auctions can be dangerously hypnotic if you aren't careful, so always be sure you establish the highest price you are willing to pay for each item before it comes up to be sold.

Before purchasing any item, take some time, go to the preview normally held before sale day. Examine all of the offerings to be sold. By doing this, you can determine the condition of each piece, plus you may find other things of interest to you that you wouldn't have noticed on auction day. The preview is a must, if you want to be successful. Leaving your bidding on items to guesswork is a very dangerous practice that will cost you dearly. Be sure you pay close attention to where each item is located at the sale, because unethical people often move the items they are interested in to a different location, and may even put good pieces in box lots with the cheaper merchandise. Another common practice is to hide quality pieces under or behind unimportant pieces.

The preview is a wonderful place and time to meet other dealers and share mutual interests. You may even find a client or two as you mingle with the people in attendance. All the time spent at these auctions is like free advertising. You should talk to everyone who will listen. Network, network, network. That is the name of the game in this business. Just being friendly to others will put money in your pocket.

There are many types of auctions such as farm auctions, home auctions and auctions where the sale is transported to a building off site to be sold. Farm and house auctions are usually found in the South and in farming areas in the West. All of these are great places to discover your treasure. One nice thing about these auctions is that you are only in competition with the other live bidders who are also present at the sale.

At most auctions there is a buyer's premium which may vary from 10% to 25%. As you bid, you must always mentally add this to your bid price so you don't exceed the total amount you can allow yourself to pay for the item without damaging your subsequent profit when you sell it.

When attending auctions, always be sure to verify that the auction company will take back anything that is misrepresented when the item is sold. This enables you to bid with confidence. If the announcer says the item is being sold "as is", you are buying the piece with no guarantee that it is not damaged, so be sure to take this into consideration when bidding.

Before the auction starts, be sure to put your name on a chair to reserve it for yourself. Be sure it is in a place where you can see the whole sales floor, including both the items being sold and the people in the audience, where auctioneer can see you. This allows you to know who's bidding against you as the price goes up so you can interpret their body language or other actions, plus you also can clearly see what you are bidding on. Don't be bashful when bidding. Stick your bid card high in the air so that the auctioneer can't miss it. I have seen people miss items they really wanted because they hesitated or didn't raise their card high enough for the auctioneer to see it. Once the item is sold, you will be told, "Sorry, but please be quicker next time."

Don't reveal to others at the auction what items you are interested in, nor the price you are willing to pay for them. They could be your competitors, or they might tell others of your interest in certain items. They, or the ones they tell, end up bidding against you.

Once the bidding starts, friendships go out the window, and it becomes a matter of "every man for himself." This may sound horrible, but you will quickly discover that auctions are dog-eat-dog until the sale is over. Afterward, it is back to everybody being friendly again.

The most important part of going to auctions is knowing how to bid. Bidding is a true art, and you will have to practice it a lot before you become proficient. Five very important principles to always remember are:

1. Do not bid more than the amount you decided on after previewing the item. This is very difficult for beginners because you always think that your next bid might be the winner. The auction house encourages you to keep bidding. They make more money in commissions and fees as

the price goes up. They're very happy to help you pay more, even if it's more than the item is worth.

2. Once you begin to bid, don't be in a hurry. Others will think you are desperate to buy the item, regardless of price. Some in the audience may bid the price up on you, mostly for their own entertainment, then dump it, leaving you paying far too much for the piece.

   You could even be bidding against the owner of the piece and be totally unaware of it. Auction houses discourage this practice, but they can't control it because the seller could be using a friend to bid the price up, and nobody would know.

3. Always let someone else start the bidding so you will know the low end of the range for the purchase of each piece.

4. If bidding starts very low and the increments between bids are small, you may want to jump bid. Jump bidding means bidding more than the auctioneer is calling for. Here is an example of how it works: An item starts at $10 and the auctioneer is calling for a next bid of $20. You may want to bid $50, making other bidders stop bidding. I have won many great treasures by stopping other bidders with a jump bid when the piece was rare and worth many times what I bid on it.

5. This is a very serious business, and you are competing with many other educated people. You have to be sure that you don't give them any advantage over you when you are buying. You can find auction listings in local daily newspapers, and other publications. Also look on the internet and eBay for live auction locations. You should be willing to drive at least one-hundred miles for a good auction, but you can often turn

it into a family event by doing other things with the family along the way.

Also, don't overlook the web sites run by newspapers in your area. They usually include the day and time of the auction, plus driving directions to the location.

Other publications, such as *AntiqueWeek*, *Maine Antique Digest*, *Antiques Trade Gazette* (in the U.K.), *Antiques & the Arts Weekly*, and *Antique Trader* are great reference material for finding auctions. They are also a great place to buy items you are interested in. They list auctions in your area as well as all of the antique shows in the country, along with many antique shops. Each week they have feature stories on auction results and special pieces that could become the next fantastic collectible. You may find things to buy or sell in their classified section, and it can be a productive place for you to advertise, once you feel comfortable doing it.

These papers are an excellent way to find individuals who may be looking to purchase or sell items you want to sell or purchase. Also important, these are people who may not be accessible to you by any other means. These publications include pictures of the items, giving you a way to recognize them if you run across them elsewhere in your hunt.

### Tag Sales

In California, you can find **tag sales** where you leave bids on the items you want to purchase. I don't like this type of auction because the sellers can use your bid to encourage others to bid higher. If you use this kind of auction, it is better to delay submitting your bid until the last moment possible to still get your bid accepted. I don't expect this type of auction to become a major part of the auction scene because buyers don't like them. However, the seller benefits by knowing the selling price on each item will be based on the customers bidding against each other, ensuring they will get the highest price a customer is willing to pay for that item.

This is an advantage over a regular estate sale were the prices are listed, and can only be reduced when an item hasn't sold. Another advantage for the seller is that the buyers don't have to be at the same location where the auction takes place.

### Antique Malls and Shops

Another excellent resource on your quest for treasure is **antique malls** and **shops**. Any time you are out and about, you should walk through them whenever you see one. As I am out driving, my eyes are always scanning the signs along the way for places to stop. When I see a new place to shop, my heart begins to throb. My excitement grows in anticipation with every step I take. You may recall the treasures both Cecil and I found in two of these establishments: Cecil, the Kentucky Derby glass, and I, the Royal Doulton mug.

Antique malls and shops are also an excellent way to keep abreast of market values for the many different types of antiques and collectibles you will be following. The biggest advantage of going into these places is that you can talk to a real person and ask questions about the markets for various kinds of items, and what direction they think the markets are going. The owners have a vested interest in this business, so they will be more than happy to talk and share their opinions with you.

Before you leave the shop or mall, be sure to get on their listing book for the items you want to purchase. If any of these items come into the shop or mall, they can then call you, putting you among the first to have an opportunity to purchase them. This also gives them an incentive to go out and find the things you are interested in purchasing, because they now have a buyer to show their purchases to.

Books or directories are available that list all of the antique malls and shops in each state. They are usually free.

With changes in technology and society's habits, I suspect that malls and individual shops will soon be a thing of the past. It takes too much time and driving to find them, and when you compare their wares to what is readily available on the internet, shops tend to have too few items you would be interested in. Still, those issues aside, storefront malls and shops can be great, if you find them on your way to somewhere else. Then they become just a short break in a trip you were taking anyway.

Another strike against malls and shops is that most of them are now selling on the internet and at auctions. This means the only things left for customers to buy in the store tend to be cheap, sub-par pieces. Consequently, many malls and shops have devolved into common second-hand shops, rather than a place to find quality antiques and collectibles.

### Private Homes

The last place we are going to study will be **people's homes** you have gained access to through advertising in newspapers, in other publications, or by word-of-mouth. What a great treat this is! No rushing around. No people taking things out of your hand. Now you can be the gentleman or lady people expect you to be. Gone are the cattle drive and stampede atmospheres so typical of the other sales you attend. You can take your time to examine each item that interests you.

Always set the seller at ease by having a genuine and friendly conversation with them, introducing yourself and establishing a relationship before you start looking at the items they have for sale. Things almost always go much smoother if you can find common ground and common interests with the seller and talk about those. Help them feel comfortable having you in their home.

Before you leave the person's house, be sure to ask if you have overlooked anything they might have wanted to sell. Then, ask if they know anyone else who has things to sell. The last thing to do, as you are leaving the house, is to give them several of your business cards to keep and pass along to others.

### Using Print Media Advertising for Purchasing

You should always look in the classified ads to see if anyone has listed things you might have interest in buying. Some of my greatest purchases have come from classified advertisements. Get your paper early in the morning, and try to be the first one to call on a classified ad.

Advertising in the paper for the things you want to buy is also a wonderful way to get into private homes. This should eventually become your most productive way of buying, but don't start advertising in publications until you have been in the business for at least one year. There are at least three very good reasons for this:

1. This will give you some time to acquire enough knowledge and experience so you can go into someone's home and accurately determine the value of the things they want to sell.

2. After a year, you will sound and appear more professional. Whenever you are in their homes, you are the expert, and you need to be competent enough to be able to honestly present yourself as such. If you seem to be unsure of yourself, they will sense it. When you can honestly present yourself as the expert, they will accept the values you place on their items. This is one area where you must not try to "fake it 'til you make it."

3. Waiting a year before you buy advertising will allow you to build up your cash reserves. Advertising fees can be expensive and a drain on your account. You'll want to make sure you've left enough money in the account to purchase your next great piece.

I have been advertising in the Chicago papers and the *Pioneer Press* for over ten years. One of the most important things to remember when advertising is to keep your ads fresh. This means the ads must be changed at least every couple of months.

There are a lot of other resources you can use to advertise, such as the *Thrifty Nickel, Penny Saver, AntiqueWeek, Maine Antique Digest, Antique Trader, Antiques & the Arts Weekly, Antiques Trade Gazette* (United Kingdom), or your local newspapers. Using your money carefully and wisely is critical. Take your time in deciding how to advertise and get the most for your money. Some advertising media are a hopeless waste of good money.

It is time to start thinking about what we will be selling, but first we must be sure that we are buying the right things. It's starting to look like it's about time to start buying and get this show on the road. As John Wayne would say, "We are burning daylight."

*Stoneware*

# Chapter 8
## Absolute Personal Integrity:
### The Cornerstone of a Successful Business

I can tell you that using my system of buying will possibly make you unpopular with a some of other dealers. Why? Because if you expect to succeed in this business, you will have to be totally honest at all times, and this can sometimes hurt feelings or cause embarrassment. Many people think some antique dealers can be a bit shady; many of them even worse than used car salesmen. They have concluded that dealers will say or do anything to make a buck.

The truth is, there are a lot of honest dealers, but as we all know from experience, a few can mess things up badly for everyone else. It's the old problem of one bad apple spoiling the entire barrel.

The reason complete honesty and impeccable personal integrity are critical to success in any business is because stable, profitable, dependable businesses are built on the network of people who recommend you to others. These people who will be recommending you to others might be other dealers, people who give your name to family members, friends of people who have purchased from you, or people who have simply gotten to know you through your years in this business.

These people, who are so critically necessary in assuring you of success in *anything* you do, must feel completely safe in telling others that you are a great person to do business with. They are like the linemen in football, they clear the way for you, the quarterback, but if you disappoint them, they can leave you all alone with nothing but a destroyed reputation.

Unfortunately, for many, the standard in the business seems to be: Make as much money as you can the first time you do business with someone because you probably won't be back. I am unaware of any other way that could possibly be more effective in guaranteeing you will be in the business for no more than a very short time.

Always remember: The efforts of many will be better in the long run than all of your efforts alone. This business is built through other people and you will always want their confidence. I have two standards of conduct that will ensure your honesty and integrity:

1. If you find something you want to buy, and it is priced to the world (general public), then you have no obligation to the seller to tell them anything regarding its value, regardless of what it might be worth.

2. If the seller asks your opinion, you have the obligation to tell him or her the true value of the piece, because you now have become the expert. When you give them the price,

you must then explain that you cannot pay that price because it is the retail value, and when you resell it, you will only get about one half of that price yourself. By always doing the honest thing, you will never have to look back behind you to see if there is anyone there who has discovered you took advantage of them.

Integrity is also important for legal reasons. If you are dishonest, there is always the risk you will be sued.

A man owned an Indian blanket, and went to a local dealer who was an authority on Indian artifacts. He was told the blanket was worth $200, so he sold it to the dealer. Later the dealer sold the blanket at auction for well over $300,000. Upon learning about the auction price, the man who originally owned the blanket sued the dealer. I understand the legal fees now have passed $250,000. I believe the law is well founded in these matters. If you hold yourself out as an expert or an authority on a particular subject, you also assume certain legal obligations. If you mistreat people, they only bad mouth you to everyone they know. Over time, this will put you out of business.

Being honest can never hurt you in the long run, even if it costs you the opportunity to purchase a piece at the time.

When I first started in the business, a woman brought me a vase to look at, and asked me to tell her about the piece. I told her it was absolutely fantastic and anyone would love to own it. She then asked if I would pay $50 for it and I said no. Her eyes dropped and she said, "I thought that you liked it, but you won't give $50 for it?" I told her no, but I would give her $750. I thought she was going to faint. You see, the vase was a wonderful Daum Nancy acid etched and enameled vase worth about a $2,000. I told her I could sell it for about $1,500. She said that she would think about it. I never got the chance to buy it, but no one will cheat her out of it again or buy it for $50.

I don't know if she ever sold it. I probably never will have a chance to buy it, but the best advertising that I will ever get is when she tells this story to others. She will become part of my team, reaching out to where my eyes can't go.

People are important in your business, so always give them the respect they deserve. Of course, I was careful to make sure I got all of her information for my records. This should always include telephone numbers, address, e-mail address, and a list of what she wants to sell or buy. These records will prove to be your best friend in finding items for others that they want to buy. As you accumulate them, they become a sales list so that if someone shows you an item they want to sell, you may discover you have a customer for it already.

### Commitment: An Important Part of Integrity

I have discussed integrity in dealing with others. But there is another, very important element of integrity. That is honesty with yourself. No matter what else is going on in your life, and no matter what happens in your life, honesty with self is an important foundation stone to personal happiness. This must be present before you can be effective in dealing with others. A critical element in honesty with self is the matter of commitment. Commitment to self. Commitment to a spouse and children if you are married with a family. Commitment to your values and what you believe in. Commitment to your business, your goals, your dreams.

You will make many commitments in your life. Some of those commitments are occupational in nature. You will either make commitments to a job, occupation, or profession, or you will make commitments to your dreams and the goals necessary to attain them.

To be truly successful in life, you must clearly define your dreams. In support of those dreams, set lofty long-term goals, but also smaller, attainable, short-term goals along the way that you can reach, step-by-step. This way you don't lose faith in your intended ultimate achievements. Then go to work to make those dreams and goals a reality.

The dream is what you want. The goal is what you need to accomplish in order to get the dream. Don't confuse one for the other.

And always remember: Your income and your profits are nothing more than a reflection of the value you have added to something that someone else was willing to acquire from you, or it reflects what they were willing to pay you for something you did for them. If you need or want to make or earn more, make what you do more valuable. It's that simple.

For example, when you find an item for five dollars and sell it for ten because that was its fair market value, it was probably easy to find, and equally easy to sell, so you added relatively little to its value. On the other hand, if you search and search, and discover a treasure for $200, then find a buyer willing to pay $10,000 for it, you have provided added value worth $9,800 to the buyer above what you paid for it.

### Treating People Properly

Try to be friendly at all times, even if you know what the seller is telling you is wrong, and the information about her grandmother's lamp is incorrect. Never intentionally insult the person, you are dealing with. Be helpful and share your knowledge freely with them, always in complete honesty.

I was asked by another dealer once why I felt I had to educate everyone on the value of the articles they owned. My answer was that I wanted them to know I had the knowledge that could help them when they needed it. Also, by sharing this information, they would tell others that they had dealt with a trustworthy person who could be of service to them. This is always about marketing yourself, and the best way to do that is by sharing what you know with others in complete honesty, and winning their confidence.

Be careful with your *time*. I have told you that it is important to be friendly and helpful, but also be constantly aware that your time is of great value to you. When buying, watch and be sure the person isn't just trying to get you to give them a free appraisal.

You will encounter people from time to time who are curious to know the value of their things, but have no intentions of selling them, so they will act like they want to sell, just to get a price. In my experience, I have found the best way for me to handle these situations is to ask them, "If the price were right, could the piece be purchased now?" If they indicate they don't want to sell, I tell them to check with other dealers, then, once they have a price in mind for the piece they want appraised, I would be very interested in possibly purchasing it. This strategy should be employed only after you have established that you will not be able to purchase the item at a fair price during this initial encounter.

> **>> Clue 18**
>
> Be careful with your *time*. I have told you that it is important to be friendly and helpful, but also be constantly aware that your time is of great value to you. When buying, watch and be sure the person isn't just trying to get you to give them a free appraisal.

Always be thinking ahead. If yours is the first offer, the seller will be able to use that offer to get others to bid higher than you. If it is sold, you probably won't even know it. I don't like to give a bid until the seller has given me a purchase price that would be accepted. Then, if I wanted to make a lower bid, I can. If it is rejected, I can still buy it at their original offering price.

If you are unable to purchase the antiques or collectibles you want while at their home be sure to tell them to call you last, after they have looked for other offers and come to a sales price before selling their quality items. This will at least give you a chance to make the purchase if no one else has offered more than what you think is a good buying price for these pieces. After you leave their home or place of business, the chance of purchasing any thing from them goes down dramatically.

We have discussed how to maintain your irreplaceable reputation as an honest Antique Dealer. Now you have to be able to place a value (what an item is worth in the marketplace in its current condition) on what you are buying. This is the time when you need to protect yourself from what the seller is telling you about the items because he or she wants to sell them to you at the highest price they can convince you to pay.

Often the seller is misinformed about their things, such as how old each item is, or the value someone has told them it is worth. Another problem you will face is the one where they have a piece that resembles something that sold for an expensive price. You must remember: Just because it looks like another piece doesn't mean that the pieces have the same value. Remember back to the Royal Doulton mug. One was worth $185 while the other was worth over $7,500, yet they both came out of the same mold. Also you must remember when someone says that this item belonged to their great grandmother, you can't let that influence you. People seem to forget that their great-grandmother could have still been purchasing things when she was in her nineties. Another thing to remember is that if something was a piece of junk one hundred years ago it is probably still a piece of junk today, but if this same piece had great value then, it may be your next treasure today.

> **>> Clue 19**
>
> Don't be deceived by age alone. Age, by itself, does not guarantee great value. But age plus a history of high value can mean a lot. Allow me to repeat myself for your benefit: *As you contemplate your purchase, always remember to buy the best you can afford.*

Don't be deceived by age alone. Age, by itself, does not guarantee great value. But age plus a history of high value can mean a lot. *Allow me to repeat myself for your benefit: As you contemplate your purchase, always remember to buy the best you can afford.*

*Daum Nancy*

# Chapter 9

## The Master Key to Business Success

The number-one key principle underlying this entire book is the simple matter of where you spend your money and the time it takes to sell your purchases. Whether you buy ten items at ten dollars each or one for one-hundred dollars, you will have spent the same amount of money. Now the item or items purchased must be sold before you can claim a profit. But the effort required to market the ten items will take far more of your valuable time than finding a suitable buyer for the hundred dollar piece. Furthermore, as a general rule, you will find the ten items will be far less valuable and yield far less gross profit on sale than the single, one hundred dollar specimen.

Buyers willingly stand in line to buy rare items, while common items sit. Low value pieces consume more shelf space and take much more of your valuable time to sell. They also leave you with a smaller percentage gain on the sale. If you test this fact, you will soon discover that not only are they a hassle to deal with, but they also typically wipe out even the small profit they are able to produce. At best, you recover no more than what you paid to buy them.

## Avoid These Disastrous Mistakes!
### The Antique Show No-Show

As you start your business, many people will ask why you don't start an antique shop or travel the antique show circuit. I can assure you from my own experience and the experiences of many of my friends that this is a bad idea. If you travel with the shows, you will have a lot of expenses your friends don't even know about. Those expenses always wipe out a lot of money that would normally be mostly profit if you used other methods for selling. A major show can cost from fifteen hundred to twenty-five hundred dollars *just for the entry fees, alone*!

The total cost to participate in any show includes:

- The cost to buy the items you sold,
- Travel expenses which include travel, food, and lodging to attend the show,
- Fees and expenses you have to pay to partici-pate in the show,
- Parking and other miscellaneous fees and ex-penses.

To find out how much money you made, you must add up *all of those costs*, then subtract that total from the amount of money you actually got paid for all of your sales while at the show. Now, subtract what you paid for the merchandise you sold, and what's left is profit, if it is greater than zero. The chances are you probably made little or nothing. You may have even lost money on the show.

So why do it? Why go to all that work? Why tie up your time and money, and end up with no significant financial gain? It makes no sense!

When you travel the circuit, you essentially spend your entire time working for the show promoters who make their money whether you make any or not, and you get paid little or nothing — or maybe worse, you lose money on the deal.

You would be financially better off to not even buy the items in the first place, keep your money, and just stay home. That's not what I'm teaching you to do in this business. But this is an excellent example of why it is important to not listen to some people who may mean well, but who don't know the business.

Also, while you are at the show, you cannot be at home where most people would rather be. You also lose contact with your base of people who are so necessary to your success, and someone else gets the opportunities to buy the really neat goodies you are missing out on.

If you are on the circuit, you also do your buying at the shows where you'll pay higher prices than you otherwise would. That reduces your profits again. The merchandise you bought can't be sold again at the same show, so you have to take it home, let it sit in boxes, and wait for the next show, usually several weeks or even months away.

The merchandise you paid too much for becomes a dead weight until the next show begins. But at that next show, again, there won't be any profit made on these deadweight pieces either, yet still, they continue to tie up your working capital. You simply cannot win at the antique show game. Their only saving grace is that you might have someone come to the show to sell their things and you will get the chance to buy them. Even then, most shows disallow these transactions.

## The Antique Store Recipe for Disaster

The next mistake that new antique dealers make is wanting to own a shop. What a mistake this is, because it limits your activity in your quest for treasures. If you stay in a shop, you can't be out looking, and so you miss out on the items that you could have found if you had the freedom to be outside. The pieces you miss, and the profit from selling them, will be in the pockets of other people who aren't waiting for these items to come to them. Yes, a few things will come through the door, but their cost to you will be too great.

As the owner of a shop, the only way you could go searching would be to hire personnel, and what a headache that is. Salaries, withholding taxes, and the other benefits employees want today are a major headache, to say nothing of the problem of having government tax collectors in your pocket looking for payroll taxes, inventory taxes, and every other tax they can invent to tap your till. Why would you want these problems?

There are many other disadvantages to ownership as well: theft, rent, insurance, and accumulating things that don't sell, so they just take up space and cost you taxes too. Always remember: Anything that keeps you from buying is your enemy, and sitting in one place waiting for people to come into your shop will be a major detraction from your main goal of buying treasures.

Imagine the feeling if you owned a shop and this happened to you: I once consigned a Picasso ceramic plate to a shop with an asking price of $7,500 dollars. The owner asked if they could display it in the front window, and I readily consented. Late one night, I got a call from the shop owner who was crying. I asked her what was wrong. Finally, she asked me to come to the shop. Arriving, I was surprised to see several police cars surrounding the store.

I was told that there had been a break-in, and my plate was one of the things that was taken. Note this: The intruder never entered the store. They just broke the large plate glass window, then the glass doors on the showcase that held my plate. They reached in through the opening created by the missing broken glass, and helped themselves to the best pieces. I was very fortunate, because I had insurance, but the owner didn't. Can you imagine how she would have felt if I hadn't had the piece insured?

Are you beginning to feel the tingle of excitement about the new business you're starting? I hope you can't wait to get out and start searching, so let us be on our way. . .

*Doulton Lambeth - Hana Barlow*

# Part V:
## Buying: the Foundation Stone of Profit

## Chapter 10
## Let the Buying Begin!

Every treasure hunter needs a good set of tools that will be useful in the search. These include *Kovels' Dictionary of Marks* and also their Antiques and Collectibles price guide, a magnet, tape measure, pad of paper and pen, magnifying glass or jeweler's loupe, a needle, several of your business cards, any other guide you think you might need, a small flashlight, maps of the area you are going to be visiting, plus cash or checks for your purchases.

In additon to the *Kovel's Guides*, other uselful resource books include *Miller's Pottery & Porcelain Marks Guide* and *Miller's Antiques Price Guide* (United Kingdom), or *Carters Guide* (Australia and New Zealand).

>> **Clue 20**

Every treasure hunter needs a good set of tools that will be useful in the search. These include *Kovels' Dictionary of Marks* and also their Antiques and Collectibles price guide, a magnet, tape measure, pad of paper and pen, magnifying glass or jeweler's loupe, a needle, several of your business cards, any other guide you think you might need, a small flashlight, maps of the area you are going to be visiting plus cash or checks for your purchases.

Additional useful resource books include: *Kovel's Guides, Miller's Pottery & Porcelain Marks Guide* and *Miller's Antiques Price Guide* (United Kingdom), or Carters' Guide (Australia and New Zealand).

Most people will accept checks with proper identification, and I haven't found this to be a problem. I always take a little cash but I don't want to become a target for robbery. Because of this, I let people know that I carry very little cash. I usually find that if I don't have the total amount of my purchase in cash, the seller will take a combination of cash and check.

We're now leaving the house with our list of places to search, and we feel the adrenalin starting to flow. We enter the first destination. What do we look for? We are here to buy, and the answer is: Everything that will meet our standards. We are looking to buy anything we can double the purchase price on, so we can complete one more step in our path to riches. We see a vase for two hundred and fifty dollars. On the bottom it says Roseville. That is a very popular pottery, so you have to look at it. But the pattern on the vase is common, and you know the price they are asking is too high, meaning you won't be able to double your money. Of course, if you think they might take a lot less for the vase, it never hurts to make an offer that will give you the necessary margin of profit.

Next, your eyes land on a Royal Doulton figurine priced at $75, and you check to see that it isn't damaged. You offer $50 and wait for the answer. They accept your offer and you are thrilled because that figurine listed for $225. Since you have only limited funds at this time, you may pass on many good items until you find just the right one. Now, on with our search for your treasures.

Sitting on a shelf, you spot a wonderful Zsolnay vase, so you take it down and examine it. Great! It is perfect! But what is it worth? They are asking $350 for this piece. Is it worth it? You have found through your research that this company is still in business, but their older pieces are quite rare. How can you tell if this is a rare piece or a common one? Good question, right? At this point you get the *Kovels' Dictionary of Marks* out of your bag, turn the vase over to expose the mark, then let the book tell you which one you are holding. Wow! The mark tells you this one was made in the late 1800's. You offer $300 for it but they say they are limited to a 10% discount, making your purchase $315.

It is at times like this that keeping your composure can be very difficult, but you manage. When you get out of the store, you just want to scream with excitement because this vase will probably sell for near $2,000! How many steps in your plan have you just taken? You can't wait to list your two new purchases on eBay or consign them to an auction and wait for the results.

You are really high-stepping now, and the world is yours to conquer. I can't tell you how you will feel once you start buying, but only after making a deal like the one above will you know the exuberance that comes from this experience.

We have finished here, so where do we go now? Maybe our next stop will be the Antique Mall a few streets over, or perhaps a shop just around the corner.

Off we go!

# Chapter 11
# <u>The Art of Buying</u>

Always remember you are looking to buy the very best you can afford. There will always be buyers for the best, while the average and commonplace sit on the shelf. I will keep hammering this home to you because it will set you apart from most dealers. It is always best to be known as a higher-end dealer, because the average person is looking for the dealer who is respected by the trade.

When people set out to assemble a complete collection, they find and add the common pieces to their collections very quickly. But after they have collected for a while, it is harder to add to their collection, because the missing, more rare pieces are much harder to find. This is where you come in. You help them find the difficult-to-hunt-down, expensive items. Your knowledge becomes important to them because you can help them find those more rare items, and once you do, they will be calling to see if you have found anything else they might want to buy. I would rather buy one rare item that is in demand, than one hundred common pieces where the profit is only marginal, at best.

### Skill is Important

You are only going to buy antiques and collectibles that are desirable in today's markets. To do this you will have to continue to sharpen your skills. Collecting habits change with time. Victorian Glass, Pressed Glass, Depression Glass, and Model A Ford cars are no longer in demand, so if you buy them, they have to be extremely cheap or extremely rare. On the other hand, American Art Pottery, Paintings, and Good Art Glass still bring premium prices, so spend your money wisely. Don't fill your inventory allowance with items that only a few still collect, even if they are very avid collectors.

This is nothing more than price being dictated by supply

versus demand — something every business and marketing student learns about in college (and remember, you are in business, so it is important that you understand it as well). If demand is high (lots of avid collectors looking for a specific item) and supply is low (rare pieces are needed to fill out their collections), the price rises. As the price increases, demand goes down due to higher cost, but the supply also increases in response to the same price rise, because current owners are more willing to sell. When demand drops and supply increases enough that they match, the price stabilizes.

On the other hand, if demand goes down due to market trends or changes, the price also goes down. Usually the supply drops too. But if sellers panic and dump their wares on the market, the price can plummet, as it sometimes also does in the stock market. This occurs commonly with "fad" collectibles such as Beanie Babies.

I am always looking to buy collections. By this, I mean multiple, related pieces in a single buy. If I am able to purchase a collection, even if it is not a complete collection, this means I can offer an average of less money per piece in the collection, but the overall total amount of money I offer will be much higher, and more likely to be accepted by the seller.

In some cases I have been able to sell off 25% of a collection for as much money as I paid for the entire collection, leaving the rest of the collection as pure profit. This is no different than someone buying stock in a company, seeing it rise enough in value that they can sell part of the stock to get back what they originally paid for all of it, so they still have the unsold stock at zero or very little cost. Now they can reinvest the original money they recovered from the sale back into new inventory.

There can be some risk in buying multiple pieces because, if you over-value them at time of purchase, the initial investment will take away a larger percentage of your available funds for needed building inventory. This will force you to limit your future purchases until the collection is disposed of, hopefully at a profit. And as quickly as possible.

When buying collections you must also always be very careful to make sure you are aware of *any* damage. I know it might take considerable time to thoroughly examine every single piece, but that is a very important must. If you discover too many damaged pieces in a collection you bought without examining each piece, you may find the lowered  value wipes out any potential profit.

By buying collections and selling individual pieces, I have sometimes been able to sell some of the pieces for enough money to meet my goal of doubling my money, while still having one or more of the pieces left over to add to my own collection. I have used this method to build several nice collections for myself which I can then keep and enjoy, or sell as a complete collection to someone else at a nice profit at a later time.

If you find one or more damaged pieces in a collection but still want to buy it, here's a general guideline: Unless the damaged pieces are extremely rare, you should not pay more than a maximum of about one-fourth of the price you would normally offer for that same piece if it had no damage at all. Your undamaged offer price is about 25% of what you think the fair retail price should be. So your offer on damaged goods should be no more than about 5% of reasonable retail, unless the item is *extremely* rare, as stated before. For example, if you are buying a collection of 10 pieces, if two pieces are damaged, your offer would be about 80% of what it would be without any damage, but not more than 85%.

## Determining the Correct Value of an Item

It makes no sense to go out buying if you have no skill or knowledge about how to evaluate and qualify what you are buying. If you don't know what an item is actually worth in the current market, you have no basis for knowing whether any offer you make is anywhere near correct.

There are many ways to test for value, but I am going to make it simple by showing you four factors to consider. These factors should always bring you to a correct price on which to base your offer to buy, with the knowledge of why it is the correct price. If you use these four factors in analyzing your every purchase, you should prove to be a very intelligent buyer. The four value factors are:

- Rarity
- Condition
- Desirability
- Price

There is much to learn about these four factors. It is best to invest the proper amount of time on each one until you feel comfortable using them to correctly appraise any given item, whether it be glassware, porcelain figurines, artwork, furniture, toys, or any other item.

### Rarity

The first value factor is **rarity**. This is perhaps the most important, but only if all the other requirements are met for gauging the value of each item. However, this statement does not suggest that rarity alone is enough to make an item's value increase substantially without the other factors. If a piece is rare enough, a collector will discount its value very little for damage. Of course, anyone would rather have a perfect piece, but if the number of these rare items is extremely small and someone wants one to complete their collection, he or she will overlook the damage. I have seen rare Asian pieces with many visible repairs go for over a million dollars.

Almost all highly valuable paintings have been cleaned or had in-painting (paint added to the piece where damage has occurred), been relined (a new canvas added to the back of the painting to add stability), or had repairs to the canvas or board itself. These restorations are accepted, and usually, depending on how well they are done or how poorly, this will be the factor in determining how much discount the buyer will expect from the price he would have willingly paid, had the piece been perfect. I will explain more about how this applies to paintings in the section on *condition*.

Common items can lose up to ninety percent of their normal value when damaged or repaired. On the other hand, scarce items often suffer only a minor reduction in value for the same problem. I have stated before, true collectors are in search of the best and they will pay top dollar if you have what they are searching for. True collectors take great pride in their collections and love to show them off to others. The more they can upgrade their collections, the prouder they are.

If you have a great piece, you can expect there will be someone who wants it enough that the money involved seems to matter very little. You often see this at auctions when two people begin bidding against each other. As the price escalates the audience starts to gasp. In fact, the price may exceed many, many times what the auction house had given as their estimated value. But, like a Roman Gladiator, the winning bidder emerges triumphant with his or her newest acquisition.

There is even a group of collectors called "completionists" who want to own one of every piece that was ever made in the collection of their choice. They are only one of the many categories of people who are willing to pay a premium for what they seek. Even museums are in the race to purchase select items, and they are usually willing to pay large sums of money to get unique pieces they want to exhibit. People pay a lot of money to visit museums so they can view wonderful collections by the greatest artists in the world, or see things such as the King Tut exhibit — a truly unbelievable experience! This is why I must stress again: "the rare is where it's at."

The clues just keep coming and here is another, so let's

talk about what isn't rare and why.

As a rule, ironic though it may seem, you will not find rarity among limited-edition collectibles or things that were made to be collected.

The reason this type of collectible doesn't appreciate is because people buy them, expecting to make money with them, so they store each one as if they were golden. Few are ever destroyed or damaged. When this happens, the large quantity manufactured remain with us forever — and in mint condition. Also these "collectibles" tend to be fad items that increase very quickly in value due to "pumped up" demand, but they have no staying power in today's fickle marketplace. The inevitable decline in value is almost always nearly straight down from their peak selling price.

If you choose to buy and sell this type of merchandise, be sure not to allow it to stay in your inventory for longer than absolutely necessary. Sell it at the first opportunity. This is called taking your profit and running, because large losses can be incurred if you are stuck with these fad items in your inventory when the bottom drops out from under them. The value on merchandise of this type is usually set by dealers, collector clubs, manufacturers, or people who are looking to make a quick buck. These people aren't interested in you making a profit. They only want the price to continue to advance enough that they can sell more and more of their product.

Good examples of these kinds of items include Beanie Babies, Hummel Figurines, Collector Plates, Franklin Mint, and Precious Moments. I could list many more but I think you get the idea. This type of merchandise must always be bought very cheaply. It is best to only buy these in large quantities so that the price per item will be reduced. And fewer total dollars you have to spend to acquire them.

A friend of mine was able to get twelve each of the Princess Di Beanie Babies when they were first issued. She asked if I would sell these twelve Bears for her. I consented. The Beanie Baby Bear, named after England's Princess Diana, was a much sought after item.

I had seen the bears selling on eBay for over $500 dollars at the time, so I felt anything near that would be a great price. They had to be shipped to me from Texas, but as soon as I received them, I listed them on eBay. I waited the full seven days of the sale, and they brought $350 each. When I called her and gave her the news, she was obviously disappointed. On the other hand, I am confident she is very happy those bears sold at that price, because I can buy that very same bear for only $15 today.

Similar situations occur with Hummel figurines. Some that were selling for $4,500 at their peak may now bring only $500. I once had a Hummel piece called "For Father HUM 87" with the orange carrots that listed for $4,500. After many attempts at selling it, I finally accepted $800. It probably wouldn't bring even that much in today's market.

I hope you are starting to see a pattern here, but I still want to tell you a few more horror stories so you can benefit from my experience without having to learn this on your own. I bought a set of twelve collector plates at an auction in Louisville, Kentucky for $400. Since the plates had sold originally for over $3,600, I felt very safe in investing just over 10% of that amount. My only question centered on how much profit I was going to make when I finally decided to sell them.

I kept the plates for about ten years, all the time thinking someday I would be pleased with the result when I finally decided to sell them. After we moved to Chicago, my wife suggested we sell a few things. These plates immediately came to mind, so I placed them up for auction at Dunning's Auction House in Chicago.

When the bidding was over and the hammer fell, the total price I received was a measly $300 after commissions. I had lost only $100 on a $400 investment that had been tied up for an entire ten years. Still, I fared much better than the previous owner who had lost $3,200 before me. Sometimes you just have to look at the bright side, be thankful for how much you didn't lose, then move on.

Remember too: You only fail when you fail to learn from your experience. Sometimes the value in lessons learned from the disappointments of life, both financially and in the wisdom gained by going through them, far exceeds the cost of the experience, whether in time, or money, or both.

Time for another clue: We aren't in this business to hold onto items while they appreciate. We are in this business to turn our items as quickly as we can and make our profits. We can't take another step along our path to success on that magical road of 31 Steps until the things we bought are sold and the money is in the bank.

> **>> Clue 22**
>
> We aren't in this business to hold onto items while they appreciate. We are in this business to turn our items as quickly as we can and make our profits. We can't make another step in our path to success on that magical road of 31 steps until the things we bought are sold and the money is in the bank.

In the collectibles market, you must continually be researching, and stay on top of current market prices. Even if you buy items at twenty-five percent of what the price guides say, they can quickly go out of date. You can still potentially lose a lot of money if you aren't aware of market changes. The value in these kinds of items can change daily, and the price guides come out only once each year. Worse yet, it takes time to create and print them, so by the time a new guide comes out, the data in the old guide may be as much as two years old! To illustrate how important this can be, imagine using stock-market reports from 18 months ago to buy stock in a company that went bankrupt, but you didn't know it!

Even when new price guides come out, they rarely reflect the drop in prices on the secondary market. The best guide to current price on any given item is always the price you see on eBay or other places on the internet, or at shows you attend plus the latest auction prices.

## Condition:
### Testing for Damage and Repairs

The second value factor in determining whether an item is one you want to offer to buy is condition. True collectors only look for the best to add to their collection, so the nearer to mint they are, the more desirable they become. Mint is when a piece is in the same condition as it was the day it was made.

Any variance from mint condition affects the value and the price tremendously. Damage of any kind on newer items renders them virtually worthless, so stay away from them, no matter what the price. For much rarer items, the value will still be affected, though to a lesser degree. But still, you will find them harder to sell than the mint ones.

The types of damage to look for include chips, scratches, hairline cracks, missing pieces, replaced pieces, dents, or marriages. A chip usually occurs when two objects hit against one another causing a small piece of the item to be broken off. This usually occurs on glass, pottery, or porcelain. On glass, these chips cannot be restored. They can be repaired to some extent by grinding, but when chips or scratches are ground out, the size of the piece is altered from its original shape, and the value decreases.

I have often found very rare pieces of carnival glass that would sell for thousands of dollars. But when I examined them, I found chips and knew that the true value was now only a few hundred dollars. Pottery and porcelain are different and the damage can be restored. However, restored pieces also have reduced values. That means, for your own protection, you must know how to test for repairs. Such pieces cannot be re-fired in a kiln, so the material used to restore them is a rubber-like substance.

One way to test for these repairs is to tap the item against your tooth. If the piece rings, it hasn't been repaired at that location on the item. If the sound is dull, it is an indication that a repair was made at that location. You must test around all edges, rims, etc. to make sure there have been no repairs made to the item.

Another way of testing is to run the point of a needle at an angle along the side or rim of the vase, or whatever you are testing. If the needle catches, you know it is a repair. The needle will slide very smoothly along the rock-hard surface of pottery or porcelain, and will not damage the piece. However, if it sticks, or if you feel a dragging force on the needle, it has found a spot of softer material, indicating a rubber repair. As before, test thoroughly, making sure you don't miss any possible repairs that could greatly reduce the value of the piece, thereby damaging your potential profit on the piece. *Always be sure to ask for permission to test a piece for repairs before actually testing.*

Scratches can be found on almost any type of antique or collectible. Scratches on glass cannot be repaired. This is also true for most metal items, but on furniture they usually can be mended or accepted because of wear and the age of the piece.

On pottery and porcelain, crack and scratch repairs can be performed as mentioned before. Therefore, you should always examine each piece carefully for restorations. Scratches are perhaps the least significant of the damages to be found on antiques. Depending on the severity of the scratches, the reduction in value may be minor, particularly on rare items.

Hairline cracks can appear on glass, pottery and porcelain, but only glass is unrepairable. To spot hairline cracks in glass, hold the item up to a strong light source and turn it slowly while viewing it from a side angle so the light is not shining directly into your eyes from the other side. If there is a crack in the piece, the light will refract differently in the location of the crack, making the crack very visible to you.

A cracked piece of glass should not be purchased. It will have very little value, regardless of its rarity. These hairline cracks can be repaired on pottery and porcelain, and now you know how to test for them.

There are many other condition problems, such as dents in metal or marriages on pieces of furniture. Marriage in furniture is when several pieces from more than one furniture item are combined to produce a new piece that was never manufactured by any company. Dented items or furniture produced by marriages have little or no value to collectors and therefore should generally be avoided.

I won't go into depth about furniture because I don't deal in furniture. Furniture is too heavy for me to lift and ship, so I leave this single category to others. However, I will give you a few rules to follow if you choose to collect or sell furniture. These rules always apply to furniture. When there is damage such as broken legs, arms, or drawers, they always substantially reduce a piece's value. Furniture is also reduced in value if there are any missing parts from it, or if the hardware isn't the original.

You should be ready to get into your tool kit when looking at furniture. Get out your magnifying glass or jeweler's loupe when looking at possible purchases. This allows you to see damage such as repairs, replacements, fake information, and poor quality in the piece. When you buy furniture, you must research it to see what it brings in when being bought in the secondary market. The hot items now are coming from the fifties and sixties (year 2007), but who knows what it will be next year. I often hear people say, "I can't believe that this piece is worth so little just because of that small damage." People will try to get you to pay too much for damaged pieces, and tell you that you are wrong. But always hold your ground. We aren't in this business to lose money. Besides, if the item is such a great deal, why hasn't it already sold?

As we continue to delve into this world of collecting, we must get inside the mind of the collector. Collectors are a unique, special variety of people who sometimes are trying to recapture their childhood, or they want to own things which are beyond the financial reach of others.

Keep that in mind as we continue our study of the effect condition has on value, not all aging signs are negative. Consider the aging of Ivory (from elephants, walruses, etc., or piano keys) when it turns that wonderful golden color which gives it warmth. This is called *patina* and is very much desired. In fact, if you remove this patina, the value of an Ivory piece drops by a huge amount, even if the item is ivory keys on an antique piano.

Other examples include the crazing (cracks in the glazing that covers the piece) on Rookwood pottery. This crazing doesn't take away value unless it is visually displeasing. Or the craculure on paintings (cracks in the paint caused by aging when the paint drys and shrinks, but the canvas doesn't). If there is no craculure present on very old paintings, you probably should be suspicious. Distress marks on furniture (marks on furniture caused by everyday use) are acceptable and excepted. The furniture is used, and if you see no marks on it, you should check very closely to make sure it isn't a reproduction.

The manufacturing process itself can affect condition. For example, as more pieces come out of a mold, it can affect the crispness of the design on glass, pottery or porcelain. After several pieces come from the mold, the later ones will lose the crispness, depth, and definition the collector is looking for.

There are many other reasons for the collector to turn away from a piece. Discoloration of the glaze on a piece of pottery (caused by the thickness of the glaze being too great). Bubbles in the glaze, making the item displeasing to the eye. There is a term used in glazing called *pooling*. Pooling is when the glaze pools or puddles in one specific area of a piece, detracting from the item's appearance or attractiveness.

One of the most serious condition problems found on toys and furniture is where the original paint or finish has been replaced. I was watching the *Antique Road Show* one day, when a man brought a piece of furniture in to be appraised. I could tell the appraisers were very interested in the piece. They examined it from top to bottom. Then they asked the owner some questions. One of the questions asked was what condition it was in when he purchased it. The man looking very proud stated that when he bought it the paint was hideous, with the ugliest red paint on it that you could possibly imagine. He told them he had taken the High Boy to one of the area's best known restorers.

After removing the old paint, the restorer found this wonderful wood underneath the old paint. The owner said he and the restorer both thought this piece had become one of the most beautiful high boys that they had ever seen. You could tell he was so proud of this piece by the way he told the story. He could wait no longer, so asking the appraiser for a value, he leaned back and waited for the answer that he was sure was going to be wonderful.

After a few moments, the appraiser asked, "First, do you want the good news or the bad news?" The owner said that he'd like the good news first, so he was told that the high boy was worth about $35,000. This seemed to make him happy, but he was still waiting for the bad news to come. I am sure that he was asking himself, how bad can it be? The appraiser then said, "You know that red paint you stripped off? It was worth about $100,000." With that said, I thought the owner was going to pass out.

> **>> Clue 23**
>
> When you have purchased an antique or collectible, you should have taken into consideration the condition and bought it accordingly. If you follow the rules we have set up, you will be able to make the projected profit you had intended from the purchase without having to do anything to it. Remember: We are looking to buy at 25% of what we think it is worth *as is.*

If a toy has some of the original paint, it will be worth more than if you have it repainted. The degree of paint loss will affect the price, but if it is repainted, the price will go down to its low point. It is just a plaything again. The condition that the piece is in when you find it is usually the way you should sell it. About the only thing you might want to clean, that won't reduce the value, is silver.

Another clue: When you have purchased an antique or collectible, you should have taken into consideration the condition and bought it accordingly. If you follow the rules we have set up, you will be able to make the projected profit you had intended from the purchase without having to do anything to it. Remember: We are looking to buy at 25% of what we think it is worth **as is**.

We are now going to discuss a class of items that are most affected by condition, and that will always be paintings. Each painting you are considering for purchase should be carefully examined to see if the condition has been altered from the time it was originally painted. The closer it is to being as it originally was, the higher the value will be. Many things can affect the value of each painting, and I will list most of them for you now:

1. *Has there been any in-painting?* This means, has there been any paint pigment added to the painting after it was completed? To test for this, examine the painting under a black light, which should be part of every buying kit. Any new paint will fluoresce because modern paints contain fluorescent substances in the pigment that are generally not present in original paints from earlier eras.

2. *Has the canvas been repaired in any way?* Watch for patching (these can be seen on the back of the canvas) or relining (adding another canvas to the back of the original painting to give the canvas integrity).

3. *Has the canvas been cleaned?* Cleaning is done by taking a weak solvent and removing a little of the finish and any dirt that has accumulated on the surface over the last hundred years. This is not always a negative to the value of a painting, and it may even enhance the value if it is done correctly. However, the person you use to clean your paintings should always be a true

professional in the field. If he takes too much of the original pigment off the painting, the value will plunge. This is called skinning.

4. *Has a signature been added?* One of the most damaging things that can be done to a painting is to add a signature on the canvas that isn't done by the artist. This shows up under a black light, and the signature will seem to float because it is signed on top of the finish of the painting. This is done to defraud the buyer into thinking that the painting was done by the famous artist when his fake signature was attached.

5. *Is the canvas attached to the original stretchers?* Stretchers are the wooden square or rectangle the canvas is attached to. If it is on a new stretcher, that reduces the value.

It may take you a while to feel comfortable at judging damage on a painting, but if you continue to attend auctions and visit museums and galleries, you will soon acquire the knowledge necessary to buy paintings intelligently. I specialize in paintings because the competition in this field is less than in most others, and the potential profit is unlimited.

Don't forget the Morgan painting that I bought for $16,000 and sold for $115,000. You can't do that well with most things, so it is worth the extra work that goes into becoming an expert in the field of fine art.

### Desirability

The third value factor that must be considered in calculating value is *desirability*. We have talked about how the past seems to become important to us as we begin to reach middle age. The things we remember from our childhood are what we would like to have around us as we can afford to buy them back, but often we will have to pay prices far beyond their original cost. Furniture that we remembered in our home as a child or toys that were our treasures — that we spent so many hours playing with — seem to bring back pleasant and warm memories.

The kitchen table the family sat around while listening to father telling those great stories may be something you might want to recapture. Paintings that hung on our grandmothers' walls, or the vases that were on her tables, give us the warm feeling that somehow she is still very near us. No wonder we want to have these things again as we can afford them, so off we go reconstructing our past. Another reason for wanting to regain our past is so we can share it with our children and grandchildren to continue the family legacy.

### Judging Desirability

There are several ways to judge desirability:

- Eye appeal
- Historical significance
- Name recognition
- Manufacturer
- Country of origin
- Familiarity

We will take each one of these in order.

*Eye appeal* is just what it says. We enjoy looking at whatever brings us pleasure. Most of us like to look at the things we collect even though each one of us will see the same thing differently. That old saying, "Beauty is in the eyes of the beholder," is still true today. This may cause you a slight problem as you are buying for resale, because you are not buying for yourself. You are buying for others, so you must see it as they do.

You must be able to look at a canning jar and see its beauty, because to the jar collector it is beautiful, and they will pay a lot of money for that special jar. Buying what is desirable only to you will limit the things that you will buy. If the things that appeal to you are not what most people are looking for, you may have to sit with your purchases for a long time before you find the buyer who has your same taste as you.

>> **Clue 24**

The rule for eye appeal is: *If the piece has true beauty, it will more than likely bring a fair price in the market place.*

The rule for eye appeal is: If the piece has true beauty, it will more than likely bring a fair price in the market place.

Another advantage to buying with eye appeal is that you won't mind having these antiques or collectibles in your home to decorate with until they are sold. In fact, I find great fun in rearranging my home every once in a while with my new finds.

The rule for *historic collectibles* is different than for eye appeal because you are buying something that brings back to the viewer's mind memories of an event or a person of significance. These rules are usually safe to follow if the history of the piece is connected to the person or event in a way that will keep this information alive in our memories.

A letter written by a president may bring thousands of dollars, but few would call it beautiful. Thus, you can see that the value of a letter, book, piece of furniture, clothing, or just a special piece that was owned by an individual can become an item of historic significance. For example, consider the cookie jars that were once owned by Andy Warhol and sold at auction for thousands of dollars. Though they brought $12,000 dollars or more at this auction, they were very common and had very little value on their own. They could have been bought on the secondary market for no more than a few hundred dollars. The only difference between them being that Mr. Warhol had not owned them, and the ones he owned came with a certificate of authenticity stating that he had owned the ones being sold at auction.

The next category is *name recognition* which comes into

play with art, pottery, porcelain and glass. It is also a factor in collectibles. People collect Hummels, Doultons, and Lladros, not only because of the beauty of the figurines, but also because of the name. These figurines will bring more in the secondary market than ordinary run-of-the-mill items. They will always have a market value, even though it might change from time to time. The same principle also applies to paintings. I have seen inferior paintings bring big money because of who signed them, while outstanding paintings by another less "significant" artist sell for very little.

Here is a clue for judging paintings: You may not want to judge one artist's work against another's but compare each artist's work against other pieces painted by the same artist.

This will not only allow you to compare the signatures of the artist (there are books that show artist signatures for comparison), but you can also examine the brush strokes for similarities in the artist's work.

> **>> Clue 25**
>
> For judging paintings: You may not want to judge one artist's work against another's but compare each artist's work against other pieces painted by the same artist.

Also remember that all artists have good and bad days, so not all of their work will be wonderful. Therefore, when buying, you should always try to find the best paintings by each artist. There are situations where paintings are unsigned but their history is intact. Therefore, the painting can be safely traced back to the painter, making the value the same as if it was signed.

As a general rule, oil on canvas has greater value than watercolors or oil on board, but not always. Some artists are known for their watercolors; others for their paintings on artist board. You will discover this clearly in your research. The name on a piece adds value to a piece, not only on paintings but also art glass [Daum Nancy, Galle,

Lalique, etc.], porcelain [Meissen, Royal Doulton, etc.], pottery [Rookwood, Teco, Grueby, Newcomb, etc.], and even furniture [Stickley].

The name doesn't even have to be the artist's. Teco pottery is a good example of what I am talking about. Teco pieces don't have the artist's name on them. Instead, they have the *manufacturer's* Teco hallmark on each item. But because of the reputation of the people who designed the company's products, the hallmark adds greatly to its value.

Koreans are buying back the antiques that were taken out of their county when they were under occupation, so this gives you a special reason to buy pieces based on *country of origin*. Another reason why the country of origin can be an exciting place to look for treasure is that, as currency exchange values change, it gives one country or the other a cost advantage in buying.

For instance when I started in the business I could buy overseas at a discounted prices because the dollar was so strong. I could buy antiques in Germany, France, England and Italy at steep discounts because the dollar was king. Also, there were a lot of imports to this country, and they ended up in collectors' hands. But today, the trend has reversed, and, with the weakness in the dollar, it has caused a huge exodus of antiques and collectibles to the countries I was once buying from.

Last, but not least, *desirability* can come from just having known these items in our past. Trends in the market place can change very quickly. That is why we don't want to carry our inventory any longer than necessary.

### Price

Now we finally come to the last step in grading our purchases: *Price*. This is where everything you have learned about buying comes into play. All the research has been done, you have formed your opinion of what the item is worth and what you can get out of it when you sell, and you are now ready to buy the selected item. It is now time to make an offer on this newly discovered treasure. You know it is fairly rare, has no damage, and the desirability is apparently there, so all that is left to do is make an offer.

The excitement is building inside you, and you are having a difficult time containing the anticipation that this wonderful item soon will belong to you. But what do you offer? This will test all of your skills, because you must convince the seller that the offer you are making is fair from the seller's point of view. The seller will have to think your opinion is credible, and that you are persuasive and honest in the offer.

By this time, you should have overcome all of the seller's objections, and have shown him that your offer is the best thing for him, so he should accept it. This is a time for confidence. The presentation should be strong and clear as you present the offer. All of your preparation will be reflected in how the seller gives his response. You are probably holding your breath at this point, hoping it will be positive.

The offer should be about 25% of the retail price you have established by combining prices of like items at antique shows, current auctions, and on the internet. After analyzing these factors, the fair offer will come to you. You will feel satisfied in making it, knowing you will have a completely clear conscience after making the offer, because you have been fair to the seller.

There is one thing that I must warn you about: If the offer is such that you think it would offend the seller, you need to do further work on your part before you make it. If your best judgment tells you the seller's expectations are too high, it is best just to tell him how wonderful his pieces are and leave without making an offer. By doing this, you leave an open door, so he can feel comfortable about calling you back after he reconsiders how badly he wants to sell his belongings.

Another way to comfort the seller is to provide him with some examples of sales for items that are identical or very similar to the ones you are attempting to buy from him. That way, he can see that you are making a fair and equitable offer. It is important to be honest and honorable in your dealings, and leave the seller feeling good about your integrity. That is of far more value to you in the long run than any money you might miss out on or lose in the short term.

Time for a clue: After the offer is made, you must be patient, silent, and wait — not saying a word or showing any emotion until the seller gives you his response. I have seen people talk their way out of buying an item they want by continually talking when the seller was ready to close the deal.

When you don't push the seller to make a decision on the spot, often the seller will call other dealers and find that your offer was more than fair. When that happens to me, I may be able to reduce my purchase price when they call me back. But never forget: *It is always best to buy while you are in the seller's presence.*

> **>> Clue 26**
>
> After the offer is made, you must be patient, silent, and wait — not saying a word or showing any emotion until the seller gives you his response. I have seen people talk their way out of buying an item they want by continually talking when the seller was ready to close the deal.

A gentleman called me, wanting to sell his Hummel collection. I figured the retail price at $32,000, but I told him I could only offer $8,500 for it. He immediately responded that there was no way he would sell it at that price; he would separate it into individual pieces first.

After giving him the names of several other dealers, I wished him the best in selling his collection. Two weeks later he called to ask if my offer was still good. Knowing that he had shopped it to numerous other dealers, I asked how many people had given him a bid on the collection. His answer was about twelve. He was reluctant to tell me, but I knew that no one had offered as much as I had, so I was able to purchase the collection. He was happy, and guess what — I had just taken another step in my plan, plus I made a new friend who would pass the word for me. Yes, as I said before, it is always best to buy when you are on location, and every attempt should be made to close the deal. But retreat doesn't always mean defeat.

I always try to make a legitimate offer, and one that doesn't look like a low-ball figure that offends the seller. By offering a ridiculous bid, you make the seller angry, and any other negotiations will come to an end with him. If the sales process comes to an end without a meeting of the minds, that is perfectly fine. You still have your money, and the search can continue.

The last thing you want to do is over-pay because the seller wasn't willing to come to your price. You will have to learn to accept rejection and not take it as defeat, nor can you allow yourself to take it personally. A rejection by the seller only means that the two of you have a different opinion on the value of the item being discussed. I usually expect to buy about 75% of the items I bid on.

Always make sure your bid is on an *equivalent* piece (essentially identical to another item you have seen) that commanded a high price, and the piece you are buying isn't just similar to it. People are always saying they have seen the same piece they are offering me, priced at such and such a price, but after doing my research, I usually find there is very little similarity between the two pieces. For example, the only similarity between the two could be that they both are vases.

One of the most important things to remember is that prices change. They go up. They come down. *I am reminding you of this again because it is important.* In general, collectible figurines — such as Hummel, Lladros, and Royal Doulton (unless they were special rarities) — dropped in value by about 75% from the year 2001 to 2006. In contrast, paintings increased over 100% in that same time period. Trends are always set by individuals' desires to own things that will reach into their hearts and make them feel good about the ownership.

For example, if interest in and willingness to pay for a class of items is based on nostalgic connection to a specific time period, that nostalgia may disappear as those interested in the period change their interests due to age. Or perhaps they die, taking their memories with them. And don't forget the adage, "One man's treasure is another man's trash." What was so precious to grandpa may end up in the rubbish bin when his children clean out his now empty, former home or apartment.

External factors such as the overall economy, recessions, and government tax policies can also affect the magnitude of trends, and to a lesser extent the direction. For example, changes in tax laws on charitable giving have made it far more difficult for museums to acquire rare art, because wealthy donors are no longer allowed to take the large tax write-offs they once could for gifts to such organizations. Yet the museums must still rely on the generosity of patrons to fund their, now, more expensive operations.

These are all factors you cannot control. With that in mind, you can see it is critical to your success that you be continually aware of what is going on in the current marketplace, not in the past. Pricing guides can be helpful when buying, but they can be out-of-date, so you must always be careful to pay attention to the other, external factors as well.

> **>> Clue 27**
>
> It is impossible to state for sure what the next trend will be or when a trend is over. But if you are aware of price movement in the marketplace, you will know the direction of the trend and you can be prepared for the movement as it occurs.

It is impossible to state for sure what the next trend will be or when a trend is over. But if you are aware of price movement in the marketplace, you will know the direction of the trend and you can be prepared for the movement as it occurs.

The old stock-market adage applies here: Don't fight the trend, because the trend is your friend. This means even if you happen to pay too much for a purchase, allowing the upward trend to play out will correct your mistake and you'll still have the opportunity for profit. But if your purchase price is too high and the trend is downward, dump the item soon or your losses will only increase as prices continue to drop.

Price is relative to location. If you buy something on the east coast, but the true market is on the west coast, the price can be very different in each place. When you buy where the market for your piece is strongest, you'll pay a higher price than if you found it elsewhere, far away from the center of activity for the item.

As you begin to actually buy items, price becomes the most important issue. Be sure that, in your mind, the piece is already sold before you buy it. Be confident that you know where it is going and to whom. Your buyer could be a retail customer, a buyer at an auction, another dealer, or even someone on the internet. For example, when I bought the Pearly Boy mug, I already knew the dealer in Florida would want it. Therefore I could buy with confidence, knowing I would have it sold very soon.

Of course, the buyer you had in mind may not want the piece. It is also important to have a back-up plan for moving the item if your primary prospective buyer doesn't make the anticipated buy.

One of the most exciting things about this business is the wait after you have placed a bid, then hearing those special words confirming you bought it. Whenever I hear those words, I always try to figure out how much I will be able to sell the item for, then look at how many steps I just took in my quest toward the top and that thirty-first step.

Once I have figured this out, I sit back and enjoy the pleasure of knowing that my future fortune is just around the corner. So will you. We know that when we reach that wonderful number, we have arrived, and there will no longer have that feeling of not being able to get ahead that we experienced when we where working for someone else. Now we are our own master, and it is time for us to enjoy the fruits of our labor and quit giving them to others.

Now it is time to review our study of buying. We started with research: Seeking information about things we might want to buy in the future by visiting libraries, book stores, antique shows, antique malls, shops, and last — but not least — the internet. By leaving common items for others to research, our time can be better spent on rarities and expensive items where most dealers fear to tread. Our study will continue on for as long as we are involved in this business.

After research, we focused on the groups or categories of items for purchase that we had become knowledgeable on, and we continue to increase the number of these items that we have committed to memory.

Next in our study was where to buy, and that includes many different places. But the one constant was: We don't waste our time and we always plan our activities so that our effort is maximized.

I always try to determine whether my time and effort traveling to an estate sale or auction is worth my while before I invest time and money to attend it. This can be done by studying the auction flyers you can have mailed to you by the auction house upon request, or by searching on the internet for information on upcoming auctions and their content. Information on most estate sales is listed in your local newspaper. Publications such as the *AntiqueWeek, Antiques and the Arts Weekly, Antique Trader,* and *Maine Antique Digest,* will have a lot of info as well as classified ads.

What to buy was next, and that is pretty much left up to you. Each one of us will naturally gravitate to different interests, but the principles still apply, no matter what we choose. One caution: *Do not limit the things you buy to items that interest **you**. Always be looking for things **others** will want, because they are the ones who will be buying it from you.* What they want is often entirely different from what you would want for yourself. What they want is important. For example, there are very few toothpick collectors in the world. Therefore you can safely conclude that committing all your funds to buying rare toothpicks would be unwise.

A buying clue: When choosing a merchandise category within Antiques or Collectibles, or whatever other area you select, be sure your chosen category includes items you can find that are high enough in upper value limits that they can always be part of your plan. Don't get trapped still buying and selling $5 or $20 items when the next step requires you to spend a $100,000.

> **>> Clue 28**
>
> A buying clue: When choosing a merchandise category within Antiques or Collectibles, or whatever other area you select, be sure your chosen category includes items you can find that are high enough in upper value limits that they can always be part of your plan. Don't get trapped still buying and selling $5 or $20 items when the next step requires you to spend a $100,000.

As I stated earlier, don't allow yourself to get stuck buying and selling only cheap and common things. That is exactly what happens whenever anyone limits the amount they're willing to invest in a buy. For example, you can't expect to sell something for $100 if you are willing to spend no more than $10 or $15 buying it (unless it's an unusual bargain). By planning to sell for double our buy price, we must expect to normally pay up to half of our desired selling price for the item we want to sell, but not more.

To make a $100 sale, plan on investing $50 to buy the item to be sold. Of course, if you have an opportunity to buy something worth $50 for $20 or $25, by all means do it, provided you are being totally honest in making the deal (in other words, the seller has willingly set the price and offered it to you at that price). That makes the purchase even more attractive. Just make sure you *never* take advantage of someone who is not aware of the value of their item when you set the price (such as a collector's naive or distraught widow). On the other hand, if the seller is an antique dealer who *should* know the value but didn't do his research, of course you should buy it if it's worth the asking price, as I did with the Pearly Boy mug.

The same principle applies at a higher level. If your next step in the plan requires a sale in the range near a million dollars, you must be willing to invest $500,000 in the buy, including any costs required to repair or perform other necessary restorative work before it is ready for sale. Just keep in mind that, as the value of what you need to buy for the next sale increases, you may have difficulty finding items valuable enough to fill your budget. If you need to invest $500,000 in the buy, for example, but can't find an item you can sell for $1,000,000, you may need to buy two items worth about $250,000 each that you can sell for $500,000 apiece. Just be careful to avoid buying larger numbers of less valuable items because you will compromise your effectiveness if you do.

Paintings are a good example of what I am talking about when I suggest increasing the value in your buys. You should consider purchasing them because there is no fixed upper limit to their value. The reality is that one can actually find a painting that could and will sell for millions of dollars if handled and sold correctly in the appropriate venue.

Another reason paintings are worth considering is that most dealers are afraid of works of art, and they don't trust their own judgment on paintings. This gives you considerable competitive advantage against them when really good art becomes available. Paintings also never go out of style, and you will find them in almost every home you enter.

Many people I meet want me to educate them about the art world so they can upgrade their home with finer pieces. I usually start by suggesting they buy real art works by listed artists, and replace the prints they have accumulated with actual original pieces. You could do the same, with the added benefit of enjoying the art while looking for a buyer.

You can also add value to the lives of people you meet by helping them find an art piece they would enjoy. Keeping records of their interests and finding suitable pieces for them can also add opportunity to your business, especially if you can sell to a private party for the same price as you would net from a sale at auction.

There are paintings available with prices to fit anyone's budget, so your customer list will vary widely. While some people can only afford a painting worth a hundred dollars or maybe even less, others willingly invest several million dollars in a masterpiece they strongly desire to own, partly for the satisfaction of owning it, and maybe partly because they expect to sell it at a good profit sometime in the future.

Are you beginning to see that to reach our goal of climbing one step after another, it can be accomplished by getting involved in the art world? No matter how expensive the next step might be in your plan, it can be satisfied by buying listed art work by established artists. Buying just one painting, if it's the right one, might get you past that twenty-eighth step — something that would surely make your day. And being able to deal in items of sufficient value, because they are available for purchase and sale, ensures that we will always be able to take at least one more step in our journey until we reach that magic number 31.

*Robert William Wood (1926 - 1979)*

# Part VI:

## Securing the Sale:

## The Art of Selling

# Chapter 12

## Selling Your Treasures

We have traveled a long way together, but for the final study we will now concentrate on selling your found treasures and reaping the rewards so carefully earned. If you have followed the rules I set out for you while making your buys, all that is left to do is wait to see just how well you did buying, as measured by the gain in value between purchase and sale.

You may recall my explaining that selling is the easy part of our trip. From our earlier discussions, you have learned to maintain the 25% rule in your buying, so the only remaining question to address is whether you will be taking one step on each item sold, or many steps.

Selling is nothing more than the process by which you decide where your treasures will bring the most money. I have found, from my own experience that after I purchase a piece, all the weight and pressure I had felt before seems to vanish like a load from my shoulders. I suspect it will soon be the same for you. Often my students call me after completing a sale and exclaim, *"I can't believe I just made 500% profit on that lamp I sold. It was so easy!"*

Those first sales will energize you so much that I may have to slow you down. Why? I want to make sure you reach your goal, but I also promised you this would not interfere with the way you are living today. Family, friends, or other people will always be second guessing what you're doing and telling you a better way, but don't let that change your commitment to the plan that has taken you to where you are. Others probably mean well, but often, as you listen to their advice, it will lead you astray, and off of the course we set together. Remember, they don't have the same facts you do.

## Setting the Sale Price

Finding the best place to sell the treasures you acquire should always be your own decision, based on research that tells you where each item will produce the highest final reward, as demonstrated by how much net cash you are able to put in your bank account after the sale is complete and you have covered any related expenses.

You must become your own best salesman because no one has more information on the items you have purchased than you. Salesman are not born. They are created and developed through lots of hard work. As you practice the skills you have been taught in this book, you will discover nobody is more knowledgeable than you. I have seen people so unsure of themselves that, even if they had bought an exceptional treasure, they didn't have the confidence in themselves to ask a price for it that was appropriate.

People in this business will always try to convince you their treasures are more valuable than yours, but don't ever let them set your asking price. You are now the expert with sufficient knowledge to decide what the realistic price for your item should be.

I never hesitate to ask top dollar for things I am selling if they deserve the top price. However, I am always realistic. If you overprice your items they may not sell, and that isn't the purpose of our purchases. We want to sell everything we buy at a fair price and at the soonest possible moment, so we can get the money back in our account and continue on with our search for the next treasure.

> **>> Clue 29**
>
> An important clue in making any sale: Remember, you can always come down on the price you are asking, but never will you be able to increase the price once you have given it. In any price negotiation, both parties have the right to offer or ask whatever they think is a fair price. If they differ, often they will compromise somewhere in the middle where both are satisfied.

An important clue in making any sale: Remember, you can always come down on the price you are asking, but never will you be able to increase the price once you have given it. In any price negotiation, both parties have the right to offer or ask whatever they think is a fair price. If they differ, often they will compromise somewhere in the middle where both are satisfied.

I have occasionally broken my own rules in the past, and these decisions have sometimes been quite costly. Allow me one example that I am not so proud of.

I had just returned from a very fruitful shopping visit at a seller's home, where I acquired several pieces of ivory, porcelain, and pottery, and I knew they were going to make me very happy once they were sold. Upon returning home, I called a dealer and invited him to come by and look at the ivory. He assured me I would see him within the next few days.

He called the next day to tell me he was on his way, so I got the items out and had them on display when he arrived. As he studied the ivory pieces, I noticed his eyes were fixed on a vase that was among the articles that I had purchased. He asked me for the price on the vase, but I told him it wasn't for sale because I hadn't had time to research it. He resumed looking at the other items, but kept coming back to the vase.

He again asked me for a price on the vase, and I gave him the same response. We were unable to come to an understanding on the ivory, but as he was leaving, he turned and said, "I am sure there is a price you would take for the vase." I had only paid $300 for it, so, to shut him up, I said I would take $2,500, thinking he would have no interest at that price. To my surprise he instantly responded, "Sold."

The knot that formed immediately in the pit of my stomach told me I had made a major mistake, and I was right. While I am not certain of its actual value, after researching the vase, my findings indicate its true value could have been as high as $25,000. More than $20,000 lost on a sale is a steep price to pay for breaking my strict rule of not selling anything until I know its true value, then, after knowing the value, choosing to discount it from that price if I feel so inclined.

The piece was a beautiful oriental vase approximately twenty-four inches tall with a wonderful design covering the entire body of the vase. But the most important thing about the vase was the way it was signed. On the bottom, it had a square of what looked like tar, with a red cross in its center. This was the artist's mark, and it was probably from a very well known artist. Being human, there are occasions when even I need to forcefully re-impose my own rules on myself, and this was definitely one of those times.

Here are some other situations you may encounter, and suggestions on how to handle them:

If a person is pressuring you to sell an item before you have done your pricing research, it might be much wiser to wait until later, then call him back with an answer.

Also, don't fall for that old line, "I am buying it for my own collection." I have been caught by that one, and sold the piece cheaper than I would have normally, only to see it show up at auction later. In this instance, I am thinking of a Rookwood vase and a person who "just had to have it." I sold it to him at wholesale, only to see it sold two months later at Treadway Auction in Chicago, at twice what I sold it to him for. Needless to say I haven't done business with him since, but he still calls, and I am very nice to him, not wanting to "cut off my nose to spite my face."

### Don't Rush Your Sales

You can safely take up to six months to sell the things you have purchased. That is plenty of time to cautiously arrange a properly priced sale of your items, while still remaining safely within the timetable we have set. However, our goal still is to sell everything as quickly as possible, while still getting the highest price we can in the shortest period of time.

We know sending things to auction can consume as much as a couple of months before they are sold, but if this is the best way to sell it, the wait will be well worth it. Don't forget the story about the Frederick Morgan painting I sent to New York to be sold because of the difference in the markets I found for this painting in other parts of the country. In Chicago it probably would have brought $40,000, but in New York it sold for $115,000. Waiting a few weeks longer to pocket an extra $75,000 was a very wise and profitable use of my time.

### Stay Relaxed

Be relaxed as you choose how and where to sell the treasures that come into your possession. The hardest work is always in finding the treasure. That part is done. Selling is much easier, but you must go about it in the right way in order to ensure that you get a proper price. You established your cost when you bought the item. Your profit is now determined directly by the difference between your purchase price and how much you receive when someone buys it. If you hurry in selecting a sales method or channel, you may err in your choice, thus damaging your potential profit.

### Who's Doing the Favor?

I have always maintained the philosophy that I was doing a favor for the people I chose to sell through, whether auctions, eBay, or others, by offering them an opportunity to sell my treasures that others want to buy. They are the ones who benefit from the commission they receive from my hard work.

But remember these agents also have expenses associated with being in business — just as you do — and they certainly deserve a profit as reward for the services they provide, just as I expect to benefit from my efforts too. That said, I do think they are beginning to get greedy.

When I started in this business, the commission rate was a simple, standard, 5%. Those same auction houses are now charging commissions as high as 25-30%, plus a 15-20% buyer's fee. By collecting a commission plus a buyer fee, these houses now are asking for up to half of the entire selling price on the pieces they auction! That is a lot of money for relatively little work, and I would have to think long and hard to justify it. The better auction houses will negotiate their commission on the finer items that are offered to them for their auction. This is why we will try to only deal in merchandise that is attractive to the auction houses. I find that most of the auction houses are just trying to make a fair profit for their efforts on the sellers behalf. But, as you know, a few bad ones can ruin the whole kettle of stew.

Even after deducting all of their expenses, the case could be made that their commissions might be clearly excessive, based on their having a moral obligation to see that all parties are getting fair value for goods or services provided to others. The morality of such high fees, or the lack thereof, is something you'll have to decide on your own.

Let's use an example of how this might work: Suppose you find a rare painting at an exceptional price, and buy it for $15,000. You then spend about $3,000 having it repaired and cleaned properly. Your cost is now about $18,000. You take it to a major national auction house where it sells for $75,000 at 20% commission. The auction house charges the buyer an additional fee of 15%, which comes to $11,250, so the buyer's cost is now nearly $86,250. They charge you $15,000 for their commission, leaving you $60,000. You did all the work of finding the piece and getting it ready for sale, and you take home a profit of about $42,000 for your trouble while the house got $26,250 or more. The auction house's fees *were over half* as much as your *entire gross profit* on the sale, even before you consider travel expenses, transporting the item, or other costs related to the sale.

You tied up your money and your time, probably for months. The auction house took the item and sold it in an auction lasting not more than a few minutes. Did you get your money's worth from their work? Did the final buyer get his? These are judgment calls. The auction house spent years building a reputation and a clientele. They spent time and money promoting and advertising the auction. They deserve a reasonable profit. But from this analysis, you can see that if they keep raising their commission rates, sooner or later the dealers and buyers will decide whether they are getting their money's worth. Then they will cast their vote by what they do with their feet.

As you can see, the market will always be searching for a better way to conduct business. If commissions get too expensive, and the dealers feel like they are merely working for the auction houses, they will find alternative ways of merchandising their items. The same is true of buyers. If they have to pay too much in buyer's fees on top of the bid price for an item, they may look for alternatives. As retail stores charge more markup on goods, more people shop online. eBay has already developed into a practical alternative on many items. Competition will always force participants to maintain good business practices if they expect to survive.

If you think an auction house's normal commissions are too high, you can, and probably should, negotiate the commission rate you will be paying. When doing so, remember that they have costs too, and their willingness to reduce rates will depend on the value of what you are selling. In many respects, the actual cost of auctioning an inexpensive item is similar to the cost of auctioning a multi-million dollar item. So if what you are selling is not a higher priced item, you will likely find them less willing to take a smaller commission because, just as you do, they prefer the high-dollar items because there is more money there.

When the dollar amount is higher, it is not unreasonable to expect any auction house to be willing to reduce their normal commission rate on such higher-value items by well over half, that in turn can reduce your cost considerably. For example, on one sale, I was able to negotiate a 20% commission down to 6%, saving me over $14,000 on the sale. That is an excellent reward for investing a few minutes to work out a better rate.

### Protecting the Sale Price

Auction houses usually set an estimated value for your pieces, and I have found, in general, the public accepts these as valid values for your items when bidding on them. This is important to you, because if the auction house sets their estimated value too low, you may not be satisfied with the final bid on your item. Unfortunately, when the hammer falls, it is to late to complain. If their estimated value is not to your liking, you will find it is always wise to simply tell them that you would rather not sell it at this time unless they can raise the estimate. In addition, always establish a reserve price on the pieces you sell, without fail. A reserve price means the item cannot be sold until the bid price is equal to or higher than the reserve amount.

### It's Your Responsibility In Dealing Auction Houses

Though many people trust the auction house to protect them, you should never leave this to chance. I consigned two paintings for sale at a local auction house and waited for the check to arrive. They had assured me these two items would bring fair prices, and asked me not to put a reserve on them, so I didn't.

When my check arrived it was for only one painting, I called, sure that it was a simple error. They told me they didn't have room in that auction for the second painting, assuring me it would be sold in the next one. I watched as several of their auctions came and went, but never saw my piece sell.

Finally I got a letter from them with a check enclosed for $150. Needless to say I was shocked. I called and asked whose painting they had sold because I was certain it wasn't mine. They informed me that it was indeed my painting, and the check was for the hammered price my painting finished at.

The painting was from the 1800's, and also by a well known artist. Its value was approximately $25,000, but they advertised it as a contemporary piece, and didn't even give the artist's name. I immediately called back and asked for an adjustment, and they promised to get back with me.

We were unable to agree on a price, so I gave them two weeks to send me a check for what I thought it was worth. Two days before the two-week deadline I had given them to respond, I got a call asking if I would settle for less. I told them unless I had their check within two days, I would refer the matter to an attorney and we would let a judge decide the value of the painting. I received a check from them the following day for about one half the value of the painting, which I accepted.

As you can see, taking the necessary steps to protect yourself is your responsibility. One way of doing this is to deal with auction houses that automatically insure your items against damage for full fair value, even if they charge for the insurance. That way you don't have to worry about them getting damaged when they aren't in your possession. If the item is damaged or lost, you are paid for the insured value. If you set a reserve price on the item and the auction carelessly sells it for less (not likely to happen, but possible), they are liable for the error, and you should insist on reimbursement at the value you used for insurance against damage. In either case, you at least get your money for the reserve price, no matter what goes wrong.

## Know Your Sales Channels
## and Know Your Item's Value

Selling is an art, just like buying. And you must convince others that you are knowledgeable and sure of the statements you make with regard to selling your items. The reason Cecil, Jimmy, and Jim were able to sell their treasures at very top prices was because the auction houses and individuals they were dealing with knew they had a very good idea what their items were worth, and likewise expected them to do very well in the market place. No one was going to take advantage of them because of lack of knowledge. Everyone knew better than to try, because there were others elsewhere who would be very willing to buy these rare pieces that they were offering if they chose to sell them elsewhere.

Be sure to keep your pipeline of items moving so that your buyers will be waiting for your next eBay listing or the next catalog with your new listing pictured in it.

As you gain experience and credibility, collectors will

begin to call to see if you have any new pieces you will be selling soon. This is a great feeling, knowing others respect your skills in searching for the things they collect, and you will find them more than willing to pay your asking prices.

By now you are no doubt asking yourself *but where do I sell these treasures I have accumulated*? My answer is, wherever they will bring the highest price. This can range from eBay, local auctions, national auctions, newspaper ads, collectors, or even other dealers.

Some of my best friends are other dealers. They have customers who are looking for the things that I have for sale, and if I am happy with what a dealer is willing to pay me for an item, why shouldn't I sell it to him? His money is just as green as the others who are buying from you. Isn't that great? Also, by having friendships with and selling to dealers, you will find they will stay in contact with you to see if you have come across anything else that might interest them or their customers.

Now let's take a look at these different marketing or sales channels, and examine the advantages and disadvantages of each for various kinds of items.

### Using Online Auctions

First let's examine the world of eBay. This is by far the largest market place in the world by any measure. When you list an item, it will been seen around the entire world by collectors, no matter where they might live. I have had buyers purchasing things I listed from every continent (except Antarctica, of course), and over twenty countries. It sometimes proves interesting when shipping to these far away places.

eBay provides a unique way for selling the many things we have acquired. Their fees have gone up tremendously, but I think they are still fair, considering the services they offer. Their fees generally range from 10% to 15%, including PayPal fees.

PayPal is a very convenient feature because they handle the payment for you. The transaction is usually handled fairly quickly, so you don't have to wait for a check to arrive in the mail, then wait additional days or weeks for it to clear your bank.

You can reduce the eBay fees by not having a reserve, and starting the auction at a low starting bid. They show your items to the world — not only with written descriptions, but using the pictures you post.

When I first started using eBay, posting items was a very difficult task, but today, even a child can do it. Once you have mastered listing, the time required to post each item should be less than ten minutes. I usually let my listings run for a week (seven full days), and I start them at 7:30, Pacific Time zone. This makes it practical for everyone in the USA to have an opportunity to bid after they get home from work.

At 7:30 Pacific Time, it is only 10:30 at night on the east coast. This gives everyone an essentially equal chance to own the item listed, and helps make sure as many people as possible will be watching the close of the auction. The more people you have watching your auction, the better your chances will be for getting top dollar. eBay is the *only* merchandising channel that can give you this much exposure.

I encourage questions on my listings because I want the bidders to be confident that they have all the facts they need for placing intelligent bids. Be very careful to answer all e-mail inquiries promptly so your prospective buyers will be able to continue their research and feel comfortable as they continue their bidding.

Let me tell you about a set of experiences that include eBay, and illustrates some of the ethical issues you will encounter from time to time.

Attending an estate sale, I spotted a stack of dinner plates. There were fourteen in total, and to my eye, they looked special. Asking the price and being told $250, I knew they had to be mine. I let a few minutes pass, then offered $150, thinking this might be accepted, given that I had spent about $4,500 at the sale already. The dealer accepted the offer, and I left the plates sitting on the buffet with a marker indicating they were sold.

As I wandered around the dining room, a lady approached the plates and asked the dealer if they were, indeed, sold. The dealer confirmed that they were, then the woman asked the price. Upon learning what I had paid for them, she asked the dealer if she would accept twice that amount and cancel the sale. I gained great respect for the dealer when she immediately declined the offer, turned away, and went into another room.

I soon entered the plates on eBay with a reserve of $450. They had been listed only moments, it seemed, before I got a phone call from a man on the east coast asking if I would cancel the auction if he would pay me more than I was expecting from the auction. [Note: You can cancel eBay auctions if you have not received a bid yet, and there are a few other reasons for cancellations.] I indicated my decision would depend on what the offer was. I didn't wait for his answer, but I told him that if he would tell me what he intended to ask for the plates, if he were to succesfully purchase them with his bid, then I would consider his offer. To my amazement he said he expected to sell them for $2,500, but the offer would only be for $1,250. I had found a honest man so I asked him where to send the plates.

I was concerned that his offered price would not be reached at the auction, and not accepting his bid would have cost me a considerable amount of money. eBay prohibits a seller from having another person bid on his or her items just to run the price up, and I find this a very dishonest practice. If eBay catches you engaging in such practices, they can permanently forbid you from using their auction services.

I usually don't stop eBay auctions, because it may cost me money if the piece would have brought more money than the offer, had the auction continued to completion.

But in this case I had to make a judgment call, and I did. While eBay doesn't specifically prohibit what I did in this instance, they do justly frown on the practice.

This clue will always come in handy: When you are working with a buyer, be sure to make him feel as if he has found a new friend. I am hoping I hear from this gentleman many times in the future, as he becomes one of my better clients.

Allow me to illustrate something else that can happen with eBay listings. I was at a lady's house and there didn't seem to be anything of particular interest to me. But as I was leaving, I spotted a small vase on the shelf. I asked if I could pick it up. [Always ask first. It makes the seller feel more comfortable when you do.] She granted her consent, so I examined it for damage. Finding none, I asked the price, and she told me $50. Even with this small vase being unsigned, I thought it was a fair price, so I bought it.

>> **Clue 30**

When you are working with a buyer, be sure to make him feel as if he has found a new friend.

Arriving home, I soon had it listed on eBay, thinking I would surely double my money or possibly even more. The bidding started, and slowly approached the $100 mark. By the next night it was over $250! Rather than keep you in suspense, I will simply tell you the final bid made me a happy man, finishing at $1,850! I was told later it might have been an unsigned Tiffany vase, but I didn't care what it was. For $50, it simply didn't matter, and I think it brought every dollar it was worth, even if it was a Tiffany. It wasn't signed Tiffany, and I know that almost every Tiffany piece is signed. Even if I thought it was Tiffany, I wouldn't have advertised it as Tiffany.

You can see that with the broad audience eBay can provide, your offerings may bring much more than even you expected. Still, as with any other sales or marketing channel, you are responsible for managing your choices, and interacting promptly and courteously with prospective buyers.

eBay Stores is another service provided by eBay for your convenience. Your eBay store is like your own web page where you can list multiple items at a fixed sales price, and eBay members can buy them directly from your store. eBay charges a fee of 10% on the final sales price for this service, which is very reasonable. The store fee is very competitive with the costs of conducting a regular eBay auction, and may be cheaper, depending upon the amount of the various auction fees.

Note that pieces in your store are not auctioned. Any sales that occur will be at the price you set in your eBay store, and people choose to accept or reject your price when making a purchasing decision. This may or may not be to your advantage, in comparison with normal eBay auctions.

Another service eBay provides is PayPal. This is the banking side of eBay where buyers can pay you as soon as the auction is completed by simply charging it to their credit card or taking the amount out of their own personal PayPal account balance on line. This is much better than using snail mail and worrying about whether your check got lost. There is a charge to you for using the PayPal service.

About 90% of my transactions on the Internet are completed using PayPal. I usually leave only a small amount of money in my account, usually keeping my balance under $100. When my balance gets larger than that, I have them transfer the excess into my regular bank account at no expense to me.

I have told you that I couldn't be in this business without the internet and eBay, but they have their limitations when it comes to meeting my selling needs. I discovered very early on that eBay wasn't the best place for me to sell expensive antiques and collectibles because they usually bring a better price at regular auctions. I will be explaining that to you later.

Lower-end and mid-range items seem to bring a fair price on eBay so most of the time I try to use eBay for most items that fall into these ranges. However, items over $5,000 seem to get discounted on eBay, probably because the prospective buyer can't get up close to the item to personally examine it before bidding. I know if I am going to buy an expensive antique, I prefer to go where it is located so I can better judge its quality and see if there is any damage to the piece. This gives me more confidence in my decision than merely seeing pictures of it on the internet.

Some people fear internet business transactions because of horror stories they have heard, which may or may not be true. While most people are willing to take limited amounts of risk, as the numbers of internet users keep getting larger, some buyers do become somewhat more cautious. One may even hear occasional horror stories about eBay, but I have never encountered any significant problems, nor have any of my friends who use eBay.

In the vast majority of cases, I think eBay transactions are entirely safe. But as I have stated earlier, if you have any doubts about any given situation, always play it safe and protect yourself, no matter where you are doing business.

There is another way of using the internet besides eBay: Set up your own web site. The site becomes your personal store where you offer all the items you want to sell, and people can view them without you being in competition with other sellers on the same page. You can leave items up for sale for as long as you want, and the description and selling price can be changed whenever you want to change them. If you have a good, useful site, people will begin to follow it to see what new items you have listed.

This type of selling is too time consuming for most people, because the site has to be updated, and new key words must be changed regularly to keep your site fresh and easily accessible to the public through search engines. Getting your site listed by search engines such as Yahoo! and Google is a constant cat-and-mouse game of trying to figure out how to use the words that get your site placed near the top in search listings. I would suggest an eBay store instead of a web site for the first few years.

Another major problem for web sites is establishing a clientele of visitors. Major corporations invest huge sums of money, just to get people to visit their web sites. The internet is not a place where you can create a site called "myname.com" and somehow the world comes running. Your own web site address is no different than listing your name and phone number in a huge telephone directory. Even if they find your name in the book, do they know why they should come by for a visit? Not likely for the vast majority of internet users.

I would much rather be investing my time and money buying, because that is your primary path to success. Maintaining a web site can be quite expensive if you pay others to build and maintain it, and with the monthly hosting costs as well, you will have to decide for yourself whether the cost versus results is worthwhile.

### Selling Through Local Auctions

Let's discuss local auctions. These are auctions located are in your general vicinity near where you live. They may be regular weekly auctions or auctions advertised only when an estate is to be sold or liquidated. I use these auctions to sell items of local or regional interest that do not have enough value to justify the cost of shipping them to the larger, national auction houses.

I also use local auctions for items when I would like to be paid very quickly, or for items that might benefit from me being in the audience. Another great thing about local auctions is that you might encounter a good buy while sitting there waiting for your items to sell. I have attended auctions where I was cashing out some of the things I had purchased, but ended up buying things that made me more money than what I was selling.

Once I was waiting for some pottery to sell that I had entered in an every-other-weekend sale at *Direct Auction*

*Galleries* in Chicago, when I spotted a small porcelain dog that I knew was a wise thing to buy. The bidding started at $20, and soon shot up to a $100. Once it passed $50, everyone but one lady dropped out, but she continued to bid. I finally purchased it for one $1,000. The dog was about four inches tall and five inches long, but it was signed Boehm on the bottom. I knew it was by Marshall Boehm, and it was also one of his rarest pieces. In fact, there were only ten of these little Scotties ever produced. I later sold it to one of my collectors for $5,000. That day, I was very glad I had entered some pottery to be sold. Otherwise I wouldn't have attended that auction, and therefore would have missed the opportunity to advance in the completion of my plan.

These auctions seem to be very social, and over time you will begin to recognize most of the people there, turning it into a great evening out. I have been taking my son with me to them since he was six months old, and the people were always disappointed whenever I showed up without Joshua. He would sleep in his snuggy on my chest as the auction proceeded, the only interruption being for feedings or a diaper change.

You will also discover the people running these auctions can often do you favors such as getting your items into the auction at the last minute, giving you a cheaper commission rate, or being more persistent when they are offering your items for sale by calling for bids on your items just a little longer than usual.

### Selling Through National Auction Houses

There is no better place to sell a really great antique or painting than at one of the top auction houses in the country. This business really gets exciting when you have a top-quality piece up for sale at auction, and the sale is being conducted by one of the top National Auction Houses in existence.

I can't explain how I felt or properly express the adrenal

rush I got waiting for the Frederick Morgan painting to be sold in New York at Christy's. It was a day I will never forget and I can't wait until I have another chance to feel that again. I know in the future I will be selling a piece for $500,000 or more, and it will possibly be another painting. That day is coming, and I wait for it with bated breath.

Christy's, Sotheby's, and Butterfield's are just some of the top houses in this country that you should consider. Just a little less known in the auction community are Cincinnati Art Galleries, Shannon's and Treadway. I have used all of these, and recommend them highly. If you have an item that qualifies for these houses, you can be assured the money will be in attendance at the auction or on the phones to help bring your item to its fullest value.

You have heard about the big buyers. This is where they hang out. The money is unlimited. There might even be museums bidding against individuals, and corporations bidding against museums. It can get really crazy!

One thing you need to know, though: These auction houses are not looking to sell cheap items [items worth not more than from $1,000 to $5,000] and they probably would only sell those for you as an accommodation, in my opinion. The items they are willing to take for sale must be of top quality, and usually completely free of any damage.

There are some disadvantages to using these houses. One is: If your piece doesn't measure up, they probably will not be able to get as high a price as you might have received at a local auction. Also, there are expenses to consider such as travel, lodging, food, and being away from home, so be sure it is worth the trouble to take your treasure to one of these houses.

## Selling by Advertising

Another popular selling method is through media advertising. I use this method only rarely, but a lot of people claim it is their best way to get the price they want to achieve for their items. By advertising in local newspapers, they get a wide viewing of their items for sale, and most of the time the transaction can be completed over the phone. There are other forms of direct sales by advertising in such publications as *Antique Trader, Antiques and the Arts Weekly, AntiqueWeek, The Maine Antique Digest,* and other collector magazines.

These ads can be quite expensive, but this is offset by not having to pay a commission on your sales. When you use this method, be sure to catalogue each call you receive, and try to get as much information as possible on what they are looking to buy and sell. Doing that helps significantly in building the customer base that will grow to become an important core part of your business.

## Selling to Collectors

Perhaps the most overlooked way to sell to the public is by searching out and finding collectors. Most dealers wait for the collector to find them, but it is very easy to find the collectors. There are entire books published, listing collectors in every category, where they live, and their telephone numbers.

A method I use when I have an item for sale is to search eBay for people who are bidding on things similar to my piece, or who have purchased a similar item on the net. With this information, I contact them and ask if they would have interest in my piece, if I listed it. I also tell them when an item is going up on eBay so that if they are interested, they can bid. If I contact someone whose name I got from eBay, I do not try to sell the item to them directly, because by listing it, open bidding is more likely to reflect the true value when the final bid closes.

This technique has worked very successfully for me, and I think it will also be very beneficial for you. It also benefits eBay because it might mean listing the item where eBay gets the commission, rather than sending it to auction.

Always be looking for collectors at the auctions you attend. Introduce yourself and share information about your mutual interests with them. Collectors should be your best friend, because they continue to provide a place for you to sell.

## Selling to Dealers

Other dealers can be a very important channel for selling your pieces. For example, the plates I sold to a dealer made a win-win for me as well as the dealer. We both left feeling good, knowing our goals had been reached.

I never envy what another person makes on an item I sold him or her. If others couldn't make money, the market would soon dry up. I wouldn't have any place to go with the things I want to sell.

Dealers are like your backstop. If you have no other place to sell the items you are holding in inventory, they provide an excellent escape for you, and usually pay you at the time of the transaction. With your money back in your bank account and having reached your goal of doubling, it is time to begin the search for those treasures all over again.

*John Lotton Vase*

# Chapter 13

## Preparing Items for Sale

This is the time when you must make sure your piece is ready for sale. To make sure it gets the best price, it needs to be prepared properly so it is presented in its best light, with nothing done to damage its market value.

Preparing a piece for sale means

> **>> Clue 31**
>
> Preparing a piece for sale means all needed repairs are made to the item, the piece is clean and has the best appearance it can possibly have, is entered in the correct auction most appropriate for the item, and you have given the auction house a proper description of the piece.

all needed repairs are made to the item, the piece is clean and has the best appearance it can possibly have, is entered in the correct auction most appropriate for the item, and you have given the auction house a proper description of the piece.

As I told you earlier, the large auction houses can be your best fiend. Here we go again with another story. Remember the Frederick Morgan painting? I am now going to tell you the rest of the story.

After agreeing to purchase the painting in Chicago for a price of $25,000, I gave the dealer a check which he was to hold until I traveled to Cincinnati, Ohio with the painting, so I could have a friend look at it and give me his opinion. My friend agreed with me about the value of the painting, but it had been relined, which would affect the value. Returning to Chicago, I told the dealer about my concerns, and explained that I could only pay him $15,000 with the painting in this condition. He immediately responded that he could not sell it for that price, but he could accept $16,000, to which I agreed. I gave him another check for the new amount, and he returned the $25,000 check back to me.

My friend in Cincinnati, Riley Humler at the Cincinnati Art Galleries, suggested I put the painting in a more valuable frame, then have it slightly cleaned, so I sent it to him to have these things done. Before long, I received the painting back, and I was amazed at the difference. I was then certain it would bring over $40,000.

Not trusting having it shipped to New York, I put it in my car and took it directly to Christy's. Upon arriving at their showroom, they questioned me for what seemed a very long time — so long that I began to wonder if they thought that the painting was stolen. After much talk, I convinced them that I truly was the legitimate owner. A month earlier, they had sold a work by the same artist for nearly $1,000,000, so I'm sure they were doing their due diligence to make sure the transaction was legitimate in every possible way.

After a close examination they suggested that I have the painting stripe lined. (The old lining would be removed and only strips would be used to give the old canvas integrity. By doing this the buyer could see that there wasn't any damage to the original canvas) I agreed to let them have the proposed work done. They also asked if I would give them permission to put it in a different frame, and I again told them to do what was needed. On auction day when I saw my painting, framed in a $100,000 gold leaf period frame, I was overwhelmed.

I was confident the auction house was going to make a great deal of money for themselves, because the painting wasn't being sold with the frame, and anyone seeing that painting in the period frame would insist on having the frame as well. I have no doubt they did.

Christy's did the research on the painting and found the advertising rights for the painting had been sold to the parent of Quaker Oats around 1900. I personally believe the purchaser of that painting got a bargain. The subject matter of the painting was two little girls jumping rope. This was a million-dollar painting in the future, but on that day, October 18, the stock market crashed and two well known auction houses found they were being investigated for price fixing. Under these circumstances, I was very happy with the $115,000 price the painting brought.

I still wonder if the painting is now back where it started — as an advertising piece back in 1900 — purchased a full century later at auction by the same company that originally adopted it over 100 years ago.

Here is one more example where a little work can pay off. Earlier, I told you about a William Gollings painting that was a treasure for me. A friend from California called and told me he had found a painting I had been searching for by William Gollings, a great western painter from Wyoming. I asked the price and he quoted me $12,500. The price was more than fair, so I sent him a check.

When the Gollings painting arrived, there were a few small paint misses and it was dirty. The canvas was also loose. I sent it to a restorer back in California where the necessary repairs were performed, and the rest is history. I enjoyed very much the nearly $30,000 it brought a few months later. This business is so great because I am sure that my friend who picked it for me made a nice commission for himself, and I couldn't have been happier with the final sale results myself.

These restorations may cost you money, but the increase in value they will add to your treasure make them a bargain. If you can buy a rare piece of pottery or porcelain, the repairs will be worth making. But on average pieces, let the buyer be responsible for them. On average pieces the cost of repair will often exceed the increase in value resulting from the repair.

*Daniel Lotton Vase*

# Chapter 14

## Protecting Your Investment

As you move up the 31-Step ladder to your ultimate objective, the value of your assets (items on hand) will increase. So will your need for proper protection of those assets against loss or damage.

### Risk Management:
### Insurance and Precautions

Controlling risk is an issue all businesses must deal with. You incur risk whenever you buy, transport or ship, repair, place for auction, or otherwise place an item where it can be lost, stolen, damaged, or otherwise harmed. As the value of the item increases, so does your exposure to financial loss. Be sure to protect yourself against any such problems.

Insurance is the easiest and most cost effective way to protect yourself, especially on high-dollar items. For small, relatively inexpensive items stored or displayed at home, your homeowners or renter's insurance should cover losses due to normal household hazards such as fire. Check with your insurance agent to verify coverage.

Whenever shipping any items, be sure to have the package insured by the carrier and keep all records of the shipment in case of loss or damage.

When placing for auction, or having an item repaired, be sure the item is insured against loss when not in your possession. If you are not sure, ask. It's your money that is on the line here.

Be sure the auction house carries insurance on any items left for sale. Make sure the coverage is for the full amount of their estimated selling value or your minimum reserve price. Most reputable houses can provide that coverage, though some may charge you for it. If you cannot get satisfactory protection, take it elsewhere for sale.

If you are shipping a sold item to a buyer, be sure to have it insured by the carrier for the full buyer's purchase price, including shipping charges. If they lose the item, you don't want to have to pay the freight, too.

As the value of your total items on hand takes on significant value, be sure you have proper business inventory insurance on your items as a rider on your homeowner's/ renter's insurance policy. The cost is minimal and the protection may become very important if disaster strikes.

Let me tell you about a great big mistake I almost made. For years, I only carried normal homeowner's insurance which would have provided only very scanty coverage on my valuable collections. However, there was a time when I was going take an extended trip, and I was worried about potential burglary or theft at my home while I was away.

I called my insurance agent and asked him to immediately insure my possessions for their true value using a rider on my regular policy. Returning from my trip, I was comforted to find I had no theft or other losses while I was gone, but decided to keep the policy rider active.

Not long after my return, a road construction project was underway outside my home. Vibration from whatever they were doing shook my house enough that the glass shelving in one of my showcases containing one of the finest collections of Marshall Boehm dogs in the entire USA came crashing down. I was greatly comforted when I received a check from my insurance company for well over $11,000, and I was even able to keep the damaged dogs, of which some were repairable.

The insurance cost a pittance — about $125 for a full year. Had I not purchased the protection for my trip, I might have received perhaps $1,000 from my regular homeowner's policy for the loss of my dogs instead of the larger amount. It was truly a sound investment. This was the first time I had purchased such coverage, and I am convinced "somebody up there" was looking out for me.

Keep accurate records of what items you have on hand, and keep copies in a safe place other than where the items are located, in case of fire or other disaster. A copy of your computerized inventory spreadsheet stored off-site at a different location, or inventory records kept in a bank safe deposit box may prove helpful. Ask your insurance agent what your insurance company recommends.

Take into consideration that the number and value of items on hand changes as items are bought and sold. Don't assume anything. Get solid advice from your insurance company regarding how to properly insure your items when in your possession or control, including in your car or at another location. That also includes how to properly document what you have.

This is definitely a time where the "Golden Rule" applies: The one putting up the gold (in this case the insurance company) gets to make the rules (of how things are covered and how claims are handled). Get the facts directly from them. Don't assume anything!

## Physical Protection

We have discussed protection against loss using insurance, but many antiques, collectibles, and family heirlooms are irreplaceable. If they are damaged or destroyed, very possibly, an important piece of history is permanently gone. Therefore, physical protection of your treasures, whether part of your 31 Steps or simply part of your life, is important.

As is so well illustrated in the story of the Marshall Boehm dogs, the entire calamity could have been prevented had I taken greater care in selecting and installing my showcase. Insurance checks cannot restore broken glass or porcelain to a previous state. They also cannot protect items from damage caused by ultra-violet light (fading) or inappropriate temperatures or humidity (cracking or mold damage). To prevent those kinds of losses, here are a few suggestions:

- Be sure showcases, knick-knack shelves, and open display shelves are securely attached to the wall, or are stable enough that they cannot be accidentally knocked over.
- Examine shelf supports to make sure the shelves cannot slide off in any direction, causing them to dump their contents onto the floor or a lower shelf.
- Be sure shelf supports are close enough to the end of the shelf that a heavy object sitting on the shelf near the end cannot cause the other end to tip upward.
- If a heavy object is displayed on a shelf, place it above or near a shelf support. Be sure the shelf

support is securely supported by the wall with connectors designed to safely carry the weight of the object. Very heavy objects, such as sculptures, should be displayed on an adequate base supported by the floor, rather than using a wall-mounted support.

- If it is an open shelf attached to the wall with no cabinet walls or doors on the sides and front, it might be wise to have a small lip around the edges that protrudes up above the top surface of the shelf so items cannot slide toward the edge and fall off due to vibration of any kind, including small earth tremors or heavy winds, or even children boisterously running across the floor.
- Slide-resistant, decorative shelf lining can help prevent unwanted movement.
- Do not store or display artwork, photographs, documents, or other items that can be damaged or degraded by light or heat in rooms or areas exposed to direct sunlight, temperatures above about 70°, high humidity, or extreme dryness. Use a humidifier or dehumidifier to address humidity levels. Window tinting is easily installed on windows and can substantially reduce ultra-violet light levels in a sunlit room. For further guidance, contact a museum curator or someone trained in preserving valuable artwork or papers.

Some of these suggestions may seem superfluous or unnecessary, and the list certainly is not complete, but in areas of seismic activity, boisterous households with active children, or other factors too numerous to mention, an ounce of prevention is worth far more than a pound of cure. These precautions certainly would have prevented any loss of my dogs, and at very little, if any, cost. In every instance, use a good dose of common sense, with a wary eye, looking for anything that could go wrong. Then take appropriate steps to prevent it.

### The Job Isn't Done
### Until the Paperwork Is Finished

Someone once advised parents anticipating a new baby in the family: If you want the baby, you'll have to put up with the dirty diapers. The same principle applies in any business. Keeping accurate and complete financial and customer/supplier records is important to the success of your business.

There are many ways to keep financial records. Exactly how you do it is up to you. The simpler you can keep it, the less time you'll be spending "pushing a pencil", so to speak, so you can have more time to go treasure hunting. Here is a relatively simple approach that works.

Every transaction involves cash flow. Cash flows out when you buy a piece. Cash flows in when you sell it. Some of that cash flows back out in the form of commissions paid for selling, restoration/repair costs preparing an item for sale, postage and shipping charges when you buy or sell an item, and other miscellaneous expenses you might encounter. When you buy an item, having a receipt you can keep on file is helpful. You should also have receipts and invoices when you sell, either in the form of an online report or e-mail, or in paper form. An auction house should furnish you with a document showing the selling price and any commissions or other fees charged, and the net payment to you after fees are deducted.

To keep this manageable, if you are a "computer geek", you can use a computer software spreadsheet, such as Excel in Microsoft Office. If you prefer not to pad the profits of large software companies, a good equivalent is available free over the internet called OpenOffice from the Free Software Foundation as part of the GNU project that is funded by many companies in the computer industry.

Even if you like computers, it is always a good idea to have hard-copy records in case of a computer failure or other problem. For that, a simple business-bookkeeping journal is also useful. These are readily available in most office-supply stores. If you are confused, a good store clerk can probably also be very helpful.

You need to record various kinds of information in that journal:

- Description of item purchased
- Name and address of seller
- Date item was purchased
- Name and address of buyer
- Date item was sold
- Purchase price
- Repair or preparation-for-sale costs
- Transportation/shipping costs related to purchase or sale
- Gross selling price
- Commissions and fees charged by auction or selling service
- Advertising or other costs
- Net proceeds from sale
- Final net profit after buying and selling
- Total accumulated net profit on sales of all items to date

By keeping these items in a left-to-right sequence across the journal page, you can easily track which items have been waiting too long to be sold, who is buying certain kinds of items, and other useful information. If you have too many buys without enough items sold, you can readily see that you need to get more items sold or you'll run short of cash in your bank account and won't have what you need for the next big buying opportunity.

The profit on each piece shows up in the next-to-last column on the right. That profit is added to the running total in the far right-hand column to show how you are progressing on your 31 Steps. It works much like your normal check register for your personal checking account.

I hope that as you total the last column on each page in the journal, the profit column, this will demonstrate to you the fruits of your labor by completing one or more steps on each set of transactions.

The last remaining thing you need in order to complete each sale is to wait to be paid on the transaction if it wasn't made in person. When you have the actual funds safely in hand, then ship the items to the new owner.

## Shipping

I normally use United States Postal Service mail for my shipping because I have found they have damaged fewer of my parcels while handling and shipping, and their rates are competitive. They also provide free shipping materials when you use their Priority Mail service.

In my case, the Post Office is very near my home, so convenience also plays a part in that decision. There are other ways to ship, including FedEx, UPS, and private carriers. If the article you are shipping is extremely large, you may need to use FedEx, UPS, or a private carrier better able to accommodate your needs. Again, be sure to adequately insure all shipments to prevent loss in case of mishap.

*Carl G. Graf (1892 - 1947)*

# Part VII:
## Returning Home:
## The End of
## A Voyage

## The Beginning
## of A New Dream

*Robert William Wood   (1926 - 1979)*

# Chapter 15
# <u>The End Of The Voyage:</u>

### Summary, Perspectives, and Conclusion

We have come to the end of the voyage, and all that is left to do is summarize and conclude this most wonderful and exciting journey.

I have done my best to lift the veil of secrecy that pervades this business, so you can gain access to it. I am sure there are many who will be unhappy because I opened the lock to what they think should be exclusively their treasure chest, but I am interested in your success, and before you can attain it, you need to know the truth about this venture you are about to embark on.

There is no college that teaches the art of buying and selling. This information has stayed in the hands of a very few people for too long. This is why I have attempted to share this with you so you will know how the most successful dealers have accumulated their fortunes.

There no doubt will be many people who disagree with my assumptions, but I have tried to be totally honest and above board about every bit of information presented in this book. I am completely convinced that if you follow the rules I have set out for you, there will be a happy and fulfilling future ahead of you.

This book is the first in a series of educational resources I will be introducing to the field of antiques and collectibles to help newcomers and others gain some experience to become more effective at developing a successful enterprise in this field. I anticipate adding more reference materials, and developing resources such as a place where you can get your questions answered, have items appraised, as well as places or channels through which you can buy and sell items.

If this journey is for you, you will become part of a new community, so that between us, there should be enough expertise and knowledge available within the community that we will be saying jointly, *"Watch out world! Here we come."*

## Now to Summarize and Conclude:

We started with a dream, but recognized that our dreams must conform with the reality of our lives today, yet still allow us the opportunity to seek our fortunes.

We also started with a requirement that your adventure must be able to start with very little money, and grow successfully from its own profits, with no need to incur debt or involve outside financial resources. This so you could develop a profitable venture without creating a big imbalance in your other household and/or family finances. It must enable you to develop a significant, and indeed, a substantial financial reward for yourself without overhauling the way you are living today. I likened this journey to going on a treasure hunt and finding enough treasure to make your every dream come true.

You were asking if such a reward were even possible, so I told you about my own personal experience, as well as, many stories of others who have tested this plan and found it to be foolproof. These are real people whom you can call or visit, and their stories were achieved without the help of someone providing them with a book containing each step laid out in a manner that would assure their success. I stated earlier that I don't believe in Santa Claus but I do believe in hard work combined with a plan that requires me to be disciplined in all I do. By consciously staying on target and following the path one step at a time, your future success will be greater than you could ever have imagined.

Remember: Most of the great wealth in the world was made by people who refused to listen to critics who stood on the sidelines taunting, *"You can't do that,"* and proved them wrong. David Schwartz, author of *The Magic of Thinking Big, The Magic of Self-Direction,* and *The Magic of Getting What You Want* wrote in his book on self-direction: *"You will never do anything worthwhile for which you are not criticized."* Every person who has accomplished spectacular feats in life has had to endure critics. Just remember, no statues are ever erected in memory of the critics. Let the dogs bark. Your caravan is moving on.

The step-by-step pathway I laid out for you is so simple it could easily pass for a fairy tale with most people, but I have news for you: I just started training a young lady named Gail, who had no background whatever in antiques. Yet with zero experience, she started out, and in her first week, she found and purchased a miniature Federal Chest for $350. Within days, the chest sold for over $1,400! She had successfully completed her first two steps in her new business, quadrupling her initial investment, leaving her with over $1,000 of profit to reinvest in new purchases, with 29 steps remaining until she reaches step 31. Ask yourself: *How many people toil away on a job for nearly* *an entire month to make that same amount of money. Yet, they keep doing it month after month even though they can **never** get ahead if they don't do something different?*

Now think for a moment: She didn't start with a penny. She began with much more. By the time she reaches Step 31, if she keeps reinvesting her profits into her business, where will she be financially? I'll let you figure it out yourself. Hint: Multiply the final number after doubling the penny each time for all 31 Steps by 35,000 (and you thought Bill Gates and Sam Walton were rich?) Do you think there is a big smile on her face as she goes about, searching for her *next* treasure?

Now you can see why money is made in business — not by putting 10% or 20% of your income from a job into real estate investment and passing most of the profits from that investment on to banks and financial institutions in interest charges. What real estate investment can double, or even quadruple its value in so short a time? Money is made buying and selling, not sitting on an investment property or a certificate of deposit at the local bank, where inflation out-runs the rate of return on your money.

If you find you still would like to own real estate or other properties, wait until you have reached Step 31, then you can buy it outright, and you get all of the money instead having a bank as your silent partner who walks off with most of the profit while you do all of the work! Of course, those who make their living in real estate don't want you thinking that way, but how much do they earn — really? That's why Napoleon Hill's book is titled 'THINK *and Grow Rich,"* not Work and Grow Rich.

You may be wondering how you can be certain of doubling your money. Only by looking at the selling prices on comparable items will you be able to sharpen the skills you need for buying and selling, and the comparable sales will give you the assurance you need. Remember: Pay 25% of what you anticipate is the correct retail price for each item you buy, and don't let others set your buying price for you. Never forget: ***compound, Compound, COM-***

*POUND.*

Next we discussed where to buy, and concluded you can buy anywhere you see or find things for sale. The greatest treasures often appear in places where you least expect to find them — even on a Father's Day trip.

I have shown you how to use this plan and the associated principles for creating income and wealth from Antiques and Collectibles, but the same process can be applied to anything. If there were no antiques, I could do the same with anything that is easily sold, whether it be sports items, golf clubs, women's clothing, shoes, books, jewelry, toys, rugs, children's clothes, or anything else I might encounter.

Always remember: You will work much harder for less money if you don't build your way into high-value merchandise. You make more money doubling your investment in one saleable $1,500 item than doubling 225 items at $5. Sam Walton made his billions selling $5 items, but look how many stores and employees it takes to run Walmart.

Another way to look at Gail's experience is to recognize that in her first sale, she was at the same level of accumulated profit as she would have been had she taken a penny and doubled it from step 1 through 17, with 14 steps remaining to reach over $20,000,000. And she did it in only one week! Either way, she is on her way to being financially much better off.

We must always buy the best that is available with the money we have in our account. We studied the places to sell and which one would be the best for different items. We also discussed who to sell to, and how to approach them.

Now it is time to turn you loose so you can go chase your dreams. My dreams were set for me by reading a children's book, but I don't know what will motivate you. Perhaps it will be reading this book and seeing

**>> The End**

Buy & Sell! Buy & Sell! Buy & Sell! Buy & Sell! Buy & Sell! Buy & Sell!

what others have done. Maybe it's simply understanding that you have all the parts of your plan in place, and now it is time to start your journey and make some MONEY!

**Daryle's Took Kit**
- Kovels' Dictionary of Marks
- Antiques & Collectible Price Guide
- Magnet
- Tape Measure
- Magnifying Glass or Jeweler's Loupe
- Needle
- Small Flashlight
- Black Light
- Pad of Paper & Pens
- Business Cards
- Cash or Checks

## Recommended Reading List:

**Mindset Books:**

*The Richest Man in Babylon*, by George S. Clason

*The Dream Giver*, by Bruce Wilkinson and Heather Kopp

*Think and Grow Rich*, by Napoleon Hill

*The Magic of Thinking Big*, by David S. Schwartz

*Magic of Self Direction*, by David S. Schwartz

*As A Man Thinketh*, by James Allen


**Reference Books**

*Kovels' Dictionay of Marks*, by Ralph Kovel and Terry Kovel

*Kovels' Antiques & Collectibles Price List*, by Terry Kovel

*Miller's Pottery and Porcelain Marks (Miller's Pocket Fact File)* by Gordon Lang (U.K.)

*Antique Price Guide 2007*, by Judith Miller

*Miller's Antiques Price Guide 2007* (U.K.)

*Miller's Collectables Price Guide 2007* (U.K.)

*Warman's Antiques & Collectibles 2007 Price Guide*, by Ellen T. Schroy

*Carter's Price Guide to Antiques in Australasia®* - 2007 Edition

*Carter's Mid 20th Century - Collectables : Design : Décor (Australia and New Zealand)*

*Schroeder's Antique Price Guide*

*Davenport's Art Refererence and Price Guide*, by Howard Moneta

*The Book of Rookwood Pottery*, by Herbert Peck

*Collector's Encyclopedia of Roseville Pottery*, by Sharon Huxford, Bob Huxford, and Mike Nickel

*The Beer Stein Book: Illustrated Catelog, Current Prices & Collector's Information*, by Gary Kirsner and Jim Gruhl

*Kovel's American Art Pottery: The Collector's Guide to Makers, Marks and Factory Histories*, by Ralph Kovel and Terry Kovel

*Miller's American Art Pottery: How To Compare and Value*

*The Collector's Encyclopedia of Van Briggle Art Pottery : An Indentification & Value Guide* by Richard Sasicki and Josie Fania

*Carnival Glass: The Best of the Best : Identification Guide to Rare and Unusual Pieces,* by Bill Edwards (Author), Mike Carwile (Author)

*The Official Identification and Price Guide to Antique Jewelry,* by Arthur Guy Kaplan

### Trade Newspapers

*AntiqueWeek*

*Maine Antique Digest*

*Antiques & The Arts Weekly*

*Antique Trader*

*Antiques Trade Gazette (United Kingdom)*

*Antiques Road Show Insider*